BERNIE ANDERSON delivers a powerful message for those who have encountered or are afflicted with pornography. He reminds us that there is definitely hope for those who have a strong desire to break out of this vicious cycle. . . . You get the sense that Bernie Anderson is one of the Lord s chosen vessels, through his book, in delivering a compelling message that no one is exempt from the addictive nature of pornography.
Jack Sunderlage, President and CEO, ContentWatch

I love the honesty and willingness Bernie has to come out of hiding. I hope many, after reading this book, gain the strength needed to break the silence.
Craig Gross, Cofounder, www.xxxchurch.com

Bernie Anderson's story is riveting, disturbing, and painfully familiar to most men . . . . This is a required read for anyone longing to enjoy the freedom of sexual purity.
Karl Haffner, Senior Pastor, College Church,
College Place, Washington

Bernie Anderson's refreshingly honest book is not a mere analysis of a problem. It is part memoir, part reference book, full of practical helps. Anderson avoids sensationalism and refuses to turn appropriate shame into bragging. You will turn to it frequently, either for yourself or for those you love.
Richard Allen Farmer, Bible Expositor and Concert Artist

To order additional copies of
Breaking the Silence,
by Bernie Anderson, call **1-800-765-6955**.

about his battle with Pornography

BREAKING THE SILENCE

Bernie Anderson

A Pastor goes Public

Autumn
House® Publishing
www.autumnhousepublishing.com
A Division of REVIEW AND HERALD® PUBLISHING
Since 1861

Copyright © 2007 by Review and Herald® Publishing Association

Published by Autumn House® Publishing, a division of Review and Herald® Publishing, Hagerstown, MD 21741-1119

Autumn House® titles may be purchased in bulk for educational, business, fund-raising, or sales promotional use. For information, please e-mail SpecialMarkets@reviewandherald.com.

Autumn House® Publishing publishes biblically based materials for spiritual, physical, and mental growth and Christian discipleship.

The author assumes full responsibility for the accuracy of all facts and quotations as cited in this book.

Unless otherwise noted, texts are from the *Holy Bible, New International Version.* Copyright © 1973, 1978, 1984, International Bible Society. Used by permission of Zondervan Bible Publishers.

Texts credited to Message are from *The Message.* Copyright © 1993, 1994, 1995, 1996, 2000, 2001, 2002. Used by permission of NavPress Publishing Group.

Texts credited to NKJV are from the New King James Version. Copyright © 1979, 1980, 1982, by Thomas Nelson, Inc. Used by permission. All rights reserved.

Bible texts credited to NRSV are from the New Revised Standard Version of the Bible, copyright © 1989 b the Division of Christian Education of the National Council of the Churches of Christ in the U.S.A. Used by permission.

This book was
Edited by Penny Estes Wheeler
Copyedited by Lori Peckham
Cover photo by Adilfa@donpolo.com
Designed by Ron J. Pride
Interior design by Heather Rogers
Typeset: Bembo 12/14.5

Printed by Pacific Press® Publishing Association
PRINTED IN U.S.A.

Library of Congress Cataloging-in-Publication Data

Anderson, Bernie, 1970-   .
  Breaking the silence : a pastor's story of going public about his private battle with pornography / Bernie Anderson.
      p. cm. — (Real life issues series)
  Includes bibliographical references.
  ISBN 978-0-8127-0462-4
  1. Anderson, Bernie, 1970- 2. Seventh-day Adventists—United States—Clergy—Biography. 3. Sex addicts—United States—Biography. 4. Pornography—Religious aspects—Seventh-day Adventists. I. Title.
  BX6193.A47A3 2007
  241'.667—dc22

                                        2007022521

DEDICATION

To my heavenly Father,
who brought me back together
and called me out into the open.

To Christina, and

To Madison, Brooklyn, and Liberty.

Acknowledgments

I want to thank the following people for their ongoing love, support, and inspiration. Without you I never could have completed this book.

My wife, Christina, my true love, for her grace, constant support, encouragement, and strength.

My daughters, Madison, Brooklyn, and Liberty, my biggest motivation for writing.

My mother and father, who taught me to love all people and to strive to be the best in everything.

My in-laws, Betty and John Boyle, who made it clear that they love me.

Mike and Gayle Tucker, two extraordinary lovers of Jesus, who taught me about grace and how to run a church.

Andy Nash, because you are the best, and I am truly honored to call you my friend. Thanks for all the time you put in on my manuscript and for believing that I could pull this off.

Mike Davis, my precious friend, who is far more courageous than I am.

Scotty Jones, for being a constant friend, for listening, and for being at the *Newsweek* interview.

Vince and Tracee Dehm, for all the laughs, listening, and friendship.

Wasatch Hills Seventh-day Adventist Church, for embracing my family and giving me the joy of serving as your pastor and friend.

Arlington Seventh-day Adventist Church, a special place that remains close to my heart.

DeSoto Seventh-day Adventist Church, for your kindness, patience, and grace through the storm.

Waxahachie Seventh-day Adventist Church, for support, nurture, and trust through the storm.

Dwight Nelson, for responding to all my e-mails.

Joe Dallas, because your workshop changed my life, and you are evidence of God's transforming power.

Brandon Cotter, for your passion to help guys with www.pureonline.com.

Heather Quintana—your call was providential—thanks for being a friend and ally.

Matthew Gamble, thanks for your patience with me and your honest input on my manuscript.

Kevin Wells, thanks for leading that prayer in the hotel room that night.

Ron and Betty Whitehead, thanks for teaching me how to serve the church.

Steve Gifford, for the courage to let me say what needed to be said.

Danny and Gina Webb, for being the life of the party and our best friends during seminary.

Gerald and Joanna, for the early-morning breakfasts with Gerald and for constant friendship.

Autumn and Jamin, because you guys are awesome. Thanks for everything.

Joel Ockenga, for seeing that God was calling me to Wasatch Hills and for your confidence in me.

Bill Kilgore, for always having an open door and inspiring my love for preaching.

Jeff and Bo Livingston, for always believing in me and supporting my family.

Karl Hafner, for reading my manuscript and giving great feedback.

Richard Allen Farmer, for your gift of music and preaching that inspires me.

Craig Gross and the www.xxxchurch.com team, for not being afraid to shake things up.

Matt and Florence Driscoll, for your friendship and support over the years.

Dan and Rose Swinyar, for standing up for me when I wasn't around.

Churches, conferences, events, and universities that let me tell my story to your people.

Everyone who replied to my e-mail with the news.

Everyone who called to let me know that you have my back.

Contents

Preface 11

Foreword 13

Chapter 1 "Daddy's Broken" 15

Chapter 2 Caught in the Web 20

Chapter 3 Breakthrough 29

Chapter 4 Turning Things Around 38

Chapter 5 My Story: Devastation and Tragedy 47

Chapter 6 Absorbing the Blow 54

Chapter 7 Going Public 62

Chapter 8 Finding Our Way Back 70

Chapter 9 Driving Forces 83

Chapter 10 The Power of Porn 97

Chapter 11 Waging a Successful Battle 110

Chapter 12 Pastor to Pastor................................125

Chapter 13 A Different Story 137

Resources 141

PREFACE

It was in the fall of 2003 that I opened up and began to talk about my problem with pornography. Throughout my life—as a boy, a young man, and, ultimately, a pastor—I struggled with pornography before finally giving in and allowing God to transform my heart. The freedom that I've known for the past few years has compelled me to share my story with thousands of people around the country. That same freedom compels me to write it all down now and share it with you.

For some time I've felt that the church (every church) needs to have a candid and open discussion about sexual integrity. In my ministry as a pastor I've found that the most common spiritual struggle—especially for men, regardless of age or background—is in the area of sexual sin. If asked, many men would acknowledge that their constant source of spiritual failure is uncontrollable lust. I have spoken with so many men, young and old alike, who are embattled, yet churches have remained mostly silent on the issue.

Because of our silence, many men and, yes, even women simply struggle on, tangled in an endless cycle of secrecy and acting out, until it comes to light in some devastating public scandal. I'm praying that things will change. I'm praying that churches will begin to talk about this issue and that lives will be transformed because of it.

The fallacy is that pornography doesn't hurt anyone else. That simply isn't true. Damage is done on so many levels. Spouses, children, and extended family members are all impacted by a life driven by an appetite for porn. It may not seem like it at the time, but there is pain. That's the potency of porn; it is somewhat subtle, even while it is explicit.

Certain words or phrases in this book may be familiar only to Seventh-day Adventists. Words such as "academy" and "Ellen White" are not meant to be exclusive or to confuse other readers. As you know, every group has its own subculture code language. This book is being published by a Seventh-day Adventist publisher, and its primary audience will be people in the Seventh-day Adventist Church. I could have attempted to make the book more for the general Christian audience, but I sincerely felt a burden for my denomination. Hopefully it will be a means of starting discussion about porn and sexual integrity and will help develop more resources. I feel that the Adventist Church has been left behind on this discussion, as our evangelical friends have published numerous books, articles, and study guides on the issue of sexual integrity.

And naturally it is easier for me to speak to the religious culture of which I have been a part for more than 20 years. I met Christ through beautiful Seventh-day Adventist Christians in Little Rock, Arkansas. My church has, for the most part, stood by me through this journey. Leaders at all levels of our church administration, as well as pastors and lay people, have challenged me and encouraged me along the way.

Some of the footnotes I've included are a courtesy to my friends of other faiths/denominations so that they can have a clearer understanding of what is going on and perhaps become more familiar with us Adventists. This journey has brought me so many new friends and allies in this battle to rescue broken people, and it would be rude of me to leave them out.

Finally, this book isn't meant to be an exhaustive handling of the issue of sexual addiction or pornography. The book is meant to share my story in hopes of getting people talking honestly about their own situation. The book is also meant to provide some information on an issue that all Christians are facing today.

As you read, you'll discover that I'm being transparent and in some cases rather blunt. When it comes to issues such as this, there's no sense in beating around the bush. Some of what I'll share may even be shocking. My honesty is not an attempt at sensationalism, but rather an authentic discussion of sexual temptation and sin. I'm convinced that this needs to be said and said now, because so many people in the church (and out) are hopelessly missing out on the abundant life that Christ promises.

There are smarter, older, and much better writers who could have written a book on this issue. But no one can tell my story except me. I believe that God will have something in here for you, and when you are finished, please write and let me know what you think. You can e-mail me at pastor@wasatchhills.org.

Thank you,

Bernie Anderson
Salt Lake City, Utah

FOREWORD

*"Carry each other's burdens, and in this way
you will fulfill the law of Christ."—Galatians 6:2.*

*T*he apostle Paul's vision for the church was that no member
would ever need to struggle with a problem alone. Every burden was to be shared with a community of believers whose loving
support would make the burden lighter. However, in order for this
vision to be realized, the church must become a place where it is safe
to share our burdens—especially the most embarrassing burdens. We
must be safe to share our secret sin and know that it will not become
a topic of conversation among gossips. We must be safe to share our
failures and know that we will not be judged. If church is *not* a place
where we find this type of support, then we must ask ourselves, Are
we really the church?

In this bold book Pastor Bernie Anderson dares us to become the
church! Bernie lays his soul bare while holding nothing back. He
makes himself vulnerable to our criticism, judgment, and rejection,
but asks instead for our support. He pleads with us to help him carry
his burden. And he asks us to help carry not only his burden, but the
burden of every man and woman who finds that they carry the same
burden. Pastor Anderson invites us to make church a place of safety,
support, and healing. He asks that we truly become "the church."

For far too long the church has shirked its responsibility to carry
burdens in the area of sexual addictions. Pornography has been the
secret sin that no one is willing to admit exists. Church administrators, understandably, have been hesitant to speak to this problem.
We want to believe that this is something that happens to those outside the sacred walls of our congregation. It could never happen to
our deacons or elders, and certainly not to our pastors or administrators. But the reality is that pornography has a deadly grip on the lives
of an alarmingly high percentage of the church's spiritual leaders, to
say nothing of those who sit in the pews. To simply stick our heads
in the sand and hope that it will go away is to forsake our sacred re-

sponsibility as a community of care and support. Ignoring the problem also gives it license to continue its evil work with impunity.

Are we willing to be bold in Christ and become what He wants the church to become? Are we willing to face the challenge and not shirk our responsibility? Do we really believe that the grace of God is strong enough to provide healing for those who suffer from this addiction? I, for one, lift my voice in chorus with Pastor Bernie's in answering these questions with a resounding "Yes! Yes! Yes!"

In order to challenge us to become the church, Bernie shares his own story of failure, struggle, and eventual victory. He provides a list of resources available to assist us on the path to freedom. But ultimately Bernie points to the only true source of healing, and that is the efficacy of Christ's grace.

I have known Pastor Anderson since he was a student in college. I hired him to work as a youth pastor in my congregation while he was still in school and witnessed the strong power of the Holy Spirit in his ministry. You can imagine my shock the day Bernie shared his secret sin with me! You will never fully understand my joy and gratitude to Christ for Bernie's healing.

Bernie's honesty has done nothing to diminish my admiration of this energetic champion of the gospel. In fact, his willingness to boldly proclaim the power of Christ to defeat Satan in this area of temptation has only increased my love for this man. His devotion to Christina and his three daughters, Madison, Brooklyn, and Liberty, is admirable, and his devotion to Christ is inspiring.

I recommend this book to you. If you, like Bernie and countless others, struggle with this burden, these pages will instruct and encourage you. If you know of someone who is beset by this addiction, perhaps you will find a new appreciation for the weight of their burden. And if you have been tempted to criticize or judge those who find themselves in the icy clutch of this sin, you will be challenged to become "the church."

"Carry each other's burdens, and in this way you will fulfill the law of Christ" (Galatians 6:2).

Mike Tucker
Speaker/Director
Faith for Today Television

Chapter 1

"DADDY'S BROKEN"

*"My spirit is broken, my days are cut short,
the grave awaits me."—Job 17:1.*

*"The Lord is close to the brokenhearted and
saves those who are crushed in spirit."—Psalm 34:18.*

Wincing in pain, I made my way through the garage door entrance to our house. My back was stiff and tight, and I literally limped through the doorway, my hand pressing against the lower right side of my back. I wish I could say that my physical pain was caused by the stress of ministry and an overcommitted schedule. That may have been partly true, but it wasn't the only reason I shuffled along. My problem ran much deeper. I had a soul problem, not a back problem. I had kept a corner of my life completely secret, and now it was taking a toll. There's only so long that one person can live as two people, and paranoid people at that! At times the terror of imagining that someone would discover my problem became unbearable. Eventually that which is hidden will bubble to the surface and manifest itself in some way. In my case, debilitating back pain was the result of years of internal struggle, of sexual compromise with pornography.

As I hobbled down the hallway toward the master bedroom, 3-year-old Brooklyn watched my agony from behind. How sad for a daughter to see her symbol of strength, her protector, helplessly limping in front of her. Now the daddy who had picked her up and tossed her in the air so many times could barely stand without support. What she saw through her innocent eyes didn't seem quite right, so she announced to her mother, "Mommy, Mommy! Daddy's broken!"

Brooklyn had made a truly profound statement. But later, when my wife told me what she had said, I laughed. "She's right," I joked. "I'm a pastor. And I'm broke!"

But I knew better. In reality I knew that her statement ran much deeper. I was broken and unwilling to seriously seek healing and restoration. Secretly I was spiraling out of control. No one was aware of my descent, and looking back on it, I don't think I was even aware of how far I had fallen. Like Anakin Skywalker, who would become Darth Vader after giving in to the "dark side," I had given in to my dark side and was headed down a path toward certain destruction. Pornography, particularly Internet pornography, had become a controlling factor in my life.

But there was more. Along with the pornography, my eyes constantly sought out the most attractive attributes of any woman I could catch a glimpse of. I was broken, all right, wounded and distraught. But I couldn't reveal it to anyone, not even to my wife. So the option I chose was to manage it in secret and pray and plead that someday it would simply go away.

Looking back, I'm sure that the seeds were sown when I was just 9 years old and stumbled across a crumpled-up page of a porn magazine while rummaging through a closet at a relative's house. (As a kid I was constantly rummaging through closets and boxes to see what interesting treasures I could find. My oldest daughter seems to have inherited the same trait, much to her mother's dismay.) I discovered all kinds of things that my parents had tucked away over the course of their marriage. The rummaging wasn't simply confined to my own home, though, and it was while I was staying at this relative's house that I found the discarded porn magazine.

It wasn't in the greatest shape. The magazine had apparently been ripped apart and thrown into a box in the closet, and whomever it belonged to never intended for it to be found by me or anyone else. But there I was, holding a crinkled scrap of a smut magazine and maneuvering the wrinkled pages to get the proper orientation of the pictures. Even then it was scintillating. I remember visiting that closet at least a couple more times to see if I could find more pieces of the magazine.

That was my first exposure to porn, but it wouldn't be my last. Perhaps it's just part of growing up as a boy in America, but it seems that every guy I talk to about this issue found a magazine out in the woods, stumbled across a porn stash in his house, or discovered something explicit on top of a trash bin. In other words, we were innocent bystanders until we were exposed to this stuff—leaving us vulnerable to future encounters.

Sure enough, the next most vivid memory I have of stumbling onto porn was finding a *Playboy* magazine in the bathroom, this time in my own house four years later. At this point I was a teenager, and as a young man with sexual curiosity coupled with hormones, I spent much more time looking at the airbrushed, voluptuous models and even reading some of the comic strips and articles that *Playboy* is famous for. To this day I remember the name, but thankfully not the photos, of the Playmate of the Year featured in that issue.

Next, a cousin managed to modify the cable subscription at my grandparents' home and unscramble the Playboy Channel. While my parents worked I often stayed at my grandparents' house, and the room I stayed in had cable TV. My older uncles still lived at home at the time, and they subscribed to all the movie channels (Cinemax, HBO, Showtime), and much of what aired late at night was rated R. I had little supervision and watched pretty much whatever came on.

I knew what channel Playboy's programming was on, and I had stopped there occasionally, straining to see through the scrambled picture, wishing I could see what I was hearing. My guess is that the Playboy Channel must have been quite expensive, so rather than pay for it, my cousin figured out a way to pirate it. Back in the early 80s, cable television required big, bulky boxes with buttons representing the different channels. The buttons made a loud click when you pushed them to change channels, so I became quite efficient at silently clicking through the channels so that I wouldn't draw any attention. Since Playboy didn't start their movies until late in the evening, it was easy to turn in for the night, only to get up a little later to catch whatever was on while the rest of the house slept.

Perhaps the most dramatic impact came from the day I found an unmarked VHS tape just sitting on top of our home VCR. Curious but somehow instinctively knowing what was on the tape, I popped it in, and my eyes were opened to the world of hard-core pornography. Someone had recorded random scenes from their favorite porn movies onto one tape. It was the first time I had ever seen anything like this, since Playboy only showed the cable versions. I had stumbled onto something that no child *or* adult should be watching—and I was captivated. Eagerly I watched as one scene would fizzle out and a new, clearer one would emerge soon after. To this day I don't know who the tape belonged to, and it was never there again.

During this time I not only discovered pornography, but like many kids entering their preteen and teen years, I also discovered masturbation. Trudging through the awkward stages of puberty, my body seemed to have a mind of its own. Masturbation soon became a real source of guilt and shame. My conscience told me that this couldn't be pleasing to God, but it got to a point where I couldn't stop myself.

As I became an older teen, I opted to stay at home alone rather than go to my grandparents' house, which fortunately limited my access to the Playboy Channel and movies. My mother allowed cable but only the basic service. But with the emergence of MTV, with its music videos featuring bikini-clad women and its aerobic exercise shows led by women in tight-fitting outfits, there was plenty of skin to take in. Sexual thoughts and fantasies continually clouded my mind, and masturbation became the normal, frequent release.

My anxiety over failing spiritually, coupled with the fantasies and habitual masturbation, ushered in a regular pattern of temptation, failure, guilt and shame, and recommitment. Private devotions and prayer times were mainly spent begging God to forgive me for indulging. I looked to the Bible and other books in an attempt to sort out how

God wanted me to overcome my urges. Yet there was a nagging sense that I'd run out of second chances with God. This produced deeper anxiety, since in my mind I was dangerously close to committing the unpardonable sin. The constant sense of panic robbed me of the peace and confidence that I so longed for as a new young Christian in the Seventh-day Adventist Church.[1] I wondered if other kids struggled with this or if I was the only one with a major lust problem.

Quietly I sought answers in the writings of Ellen G. White.[2] I thought that perhaps a remedy lay in something she wrote. Books such as *Steps to Christ*[3] and *Messages to Young People*[4] did help me spiritually. I learned that she called masturbation self-abuse and that apparently it was a problem for men in the church back in her day as well. I'll spend more time on the subject of masturbation in a later chapter.

Still struggling to gain a level of purity, I mustered up enough courage to go to my pastor. We sat down one day after a morning chapel at our church school, and I confessed that I was having trouble with lust. Honestly I cannot recall what he told me. While I don't remember walking away from the conversation with anything significantly helpful, I can say that just sitting down and having an adult male to talk to provided me with a great deal of comfort.

The early exposure to porn had done its damage, but I would come to find many years later that pornography is only a symptom of something deeper. Porn works much like Spackle on a wall—it's merely a quick way to patch a hole, to cover up brokenness. Spackle is OK for walls but doesn't work for our souls. It would be more than 20 years later (and a lot of attempted Spackle) before I had enough courage to sit down with another pastor and admit that for years my entire life had been affected by lust that had grown out of control.

---

[1] Officially established in 1863, it is now a denomination of more than 1 million in the United States and 14 million worldwide.

[2] Ellen White was an inspired writer and early pioneer of the Seventh-day Adventist Church.

[3] A book written by Ellen White providing guidance on how to begin a relationship with Jesus Christ.

[4] A book that compiles writings of Ellen White that were targeted to teens and young adults. It was specifically designed to give spiritual guidance to youth.

Chapter 2

Caught in the Web

"I do not understand what I do. For what I want to do I do not do, but what I hate I do. And if I do what I do not want to do, I agree that the law is good. As it is, it is no longer I myself who do it, but it is sin living in me. I know that nothing good lives in me, that is, in my sinful nature. For I have the desire to do what is good, but I cannot carry it out. For what I do is not the good I want to do; no, the evil I do not want to do—this I keep on doing. Now if I do what I do not want to do, it is no longer I who do it, but it is sin living in me that does it."
—Romans 7:15-20.

During my time in academy[1] and college I was extremely busy, and thankfully it didn't allow me much time to seek out porn. Any major setbacks came during leaves or vacations from school when I was home alone. Even then, I attempted to keep myself occupied with other things in an effort to not give in to my urges. Besides that, I sensed a real call to be a pastor, and I couldn't imagine that God would be pleased with a pastor who looked at porn.

My summers were spent heavily involved in summer camp ministry, spending anywhere from eight to 10 weeks at camp. Summer camp provided a tremendous time for spiritual connection and growth for me. Sensing that God was calling me to youth ministry, I appreciated that summer camp gave me the opportunity to gain valuable experience and demonstrate leadership potential. The camp I worked at was a beautiful place situated along a massive

20

lake where I learned to love waterskiing. I built friendships with staff and campers that have endured over the years, and even today I hold close to my heart great memories from those summers. Working there, I had very little time or opportunity to look at pornography, but I knew that when I returned home at the end of the summer, I'd be faced with the same temptation again.

My calling to ministry had come several years earlier, shortly after I became a Christian. I felt comfortable in the church and demonstrated a great deal of enthusiasm and energy when leading out in various programs. It always bugged me that the other students seemed more timid about their faith, and yet most of them had been part of it for longer than I had. I wanted God to use me, so I determined in my own mind that I was going to bring some youthful energy and enthusiasm to being a Christian. Because of this I was often given spiritual leadership roles and asked to be up front for youth programs. Eventually people began to suggest that God could use me as a pastor. Further confirmation came when a guest speaker visited our church school to do a presentation on the negative spiritual impact of rock music. I connected with him easily and assisted him with his sound check by standing at the podium and testing his mic. Later he expressed to me that when I was up at the mike, he envisioned me becoming a "powerful preacher for God."

In academy I was seen as a spiritual leader on campus and the "good guy" who was going to be a pastor. Even so, I was able to avoid the typical stereotypes associated with anyone who wanted to be a pastor and was seen as a cool religious guy, which allowed me to remain in the "in" crowd. I earned the respect and trust of the school administration and yet remained popular with the student body. During my senior year I served as the religious vice president[2] of the Student Association as well as head resident assistant with the responsibility of monitoring the junior/senior hall in the dormitory. In the two years that I was in academy, I can recall only one instance that porn infiltrated our dorm. Late in my senior year one of the students brought his porn video down to the TV room and started watching it. Word spread pretty quickly through the halls, and I went down to investigate what was going on. I peered in through the door, glancing toward the TV, and saw a small group of guys totally engrossed in a hard-core porn movie. I wish I could say that right then and there I put an end to it, but I didn't. I had to preserve my "cool religious guy" image, so I smiled, shook my head in disbelief, and turned and walked away.

The same popularity that I enjoyed in academy seemed to carry over to college. I was well-liked and well-known by many. Still sensing God's calling to be a pastor, I enrolled as a theology major. Once again not wanting to be saddled with the stereotypes often given to "theo" majors, I felt it was important to become friends with as many students as possible. I was involved in sports, playing for both the basketball and baseball competitive teams as well as being the captain of the acro-gymnastics team.

While sitting in a student missionary dedication vespers during my sophomore year, I felt God leading me to take off the next year of school and serve as a student missionary (SM) to Korea. The year started out rather challenging. I had enjoyed becoming acquainted with other SMs from the different Adventist colleges during our mandatory orientation in Hawaii. But once I got to Korea, a heavy dose of culture shock set in. I was completely disoriented and wanted to come home. My sponsoring college got wind of my intentions to leave my new post and called me up and encouraged me to stay. Their persuasive words convinced me that I should stay, and eventually I recovered from the culture shock and enjoyed the rest of the year. Since I lived with three other student missionaries and we were extremely busy teaching English and giving Bible studies, I went an entire year without pornography.

I returned from my year abroad firmly convinced that I would devote my life to pastoral ministry. During this same time (my junior year), my friends convinced me that I should run for Student Body president. At first I was intimidated by the thought of being in such a campus leadership position, but later I became convinced that it was an opportunity to strongly impact the campus spiritually. So I campaigned and won the election to serve as president of the Student Body for the coming school year.

Around the same time, I was contacted by a local church that was interested in my serving as their youth pastor. I was required by the theology department to be involved in a church during my senior year anyway, and seeing it as an opportunity for real ministry experience as well as a possibility for future employment, I accepted the position without hesitation.

It was during my junior year also that I met the young woman who eventually became my wife. Christina caught my eye as I was eating lunch in the cafeteria one day. Even though I lived off campus, as Student Body president I felt it was important to be seen in the cafeteria eating the same food other students had to endure. I noted the time of day she was there, and I planned to make sure I was eating in the cafeteria at the same time the next day. Eventually our paths did cross again, and this time I asked her out every day for the next week! Our relationship grew, and I eventually proposed to her.

My senior year was quite busy. I was engaged, so there was the wedding and honeymoon to consider, as well as graduation and life beyond that. I was serving as a youth pastor in a large ministry and also trying to keep up with my responsibilities as Student Body president—not to mention academics. At the same time, a secret was an integral part of my life. Pornography was still a constant temptation, and while I wanted to confess my ongoing battle to Christina, I feared that she might quickly drop me and run the other way. And if I told anyone else, I ran the risk of others finding out. The reputation I had built, along with the trust and popularity I enjoyed, would all come crashing down.

The church I served in during my senior year was a dynamic, vibrant, and growing church lead by a husband and wife pastoral team. Under their guidance the church became very popular among college students. I felt right at home there, and the youth and adult members quickly embraced me. And through the leadership of the senior pastor, my name was given to the local denominational office to be considered for full-time employment as their youth pastor.

But there was only one problem. I am African-American, and this was a largely Caucasian conference. Apparently the denominational leadership was hesitant to hire me for fear that it might be detrimental to my future career as a pastor. This sounded ridiculous to the church and to me, but the conference administration wouldn't budge. Then something interesting happened. To this day I believe it was God's providential workings. Within a span of four months the administration that refused to hire me was no longer there. Officers retired or were assigned to new territories, and a new administration came in. The church quickly approached the new administration with the same proposal, and this time I was hired as their youth pastor. For me it was further affirmation that indeed God was calling me to serve in pastoral ministry.

In 1994 I graduated from college, Christina and I married, and I entered full-time youth ministry at the Arlington, Texas, Seventh-day Adventist Church. Like so many guys who struggle with porn, I bought into the idea that once I was married and could legitimately fulfill my sexual urges, the desire for pornography would fade. But that wasn't the case. I probably lasted about a month before I found myself in a regular video store searching for "hard R" or cable version porn movies while Christina was away at work. Once again I was in that familiar place of being hounded by this longtime nemesis. At times I was so desperate to view it that I actually sneaked into the church with my rented video, secretly watching it on one of the classroom TVs or in the audiovisual room that was located in a secluded place.

While privately I gave in to temptation, outwardly it seemed that God was blessing my ministry in spite of my secret destructive sin. As a youth pastor, I knew that what I was doing was wrong, but there didn't seem to be any way to honestly deal with it. Daily I confessed and repented of my sin, only to give in to temptation a week or so later. Before preaching I confessed and repented of my sin, asking God to forgive me and grant me His mercy as I spoke. There was never a time that I didn't understand the severity of my sin problem. I knew that it was an affront to God and likely a major hindrance to my personal relationship with Him. There were times when I desperately considered telling someone in hopes that I might find some help. I grew weary of the constant battle to maintain two lives. But I found myself never really able to shake the monkey off my back, even while serving as a pastor.

Around 1996 I was introduced to the Internet by one of the teenagers in my youth group. Knowing that I was somewhat of a news junkie, he showed me how I could get constant Associated Press updates via the World Wide Web. It wasn't long before I had a dial-up account and could regularly surf the Web on my own. Soon I began to hear that porn was becoming a major industry on the Internet. Initially I was turned off by the idea of looking at porn through my computer screen. I didn't understand how it could be that appealing. It sounded rather cheesy to me. With my lack of familiarity with the Web at this time, I wasn't even quite sure how to access porn online. But my curiosity was pricked, and before long I found myself searching for adult Web sites to catch a glimpse of what the Web had to offer.

In 1997, after serving for three years as a youth pastor, I was assigned to go to the seminary, where I would work on a Master of Divinity degree. We had put this part of my career on hold for three years—one year longer than is traditionally allowed for a preseminary intern serving in a local church. We tearfully said our goodbyes to the church we had grown to love and made our way to the Andrews University Theological Seminary in Berrien Springs, Michigan.

In one way I looked forward to going, anticipating a time of rest from the grind of local church ministry and eagerly longing for a time of being porn-free, or at least a time when the temptation wouldn't be so intense. But that wasn't the case. Before long I found a video store that carried a few cable version porn movies in the special-interest section of the store. Again I found myself giving in when I had time at home alone. I remember thinking to myself that I was taking an incredible risk by renting adult videos from that store. In such a small town, a student or even a professor could have easily spotted me.

What I had hoped to be a relatively calm two and a half years of spending time with Christina and our 1-year-old daughter, Madison, turned into an intense time of ministry and study. Shortly after I arrived at the seminary, a longtime mentor and friend whom I'd worked for at summer camp asked me to consider serving as the nighttime program director for the upcoming international Pathfinder[3] Camporee.[4] This event is sponsored by the highest administrative level of the Adventist Church in North America every five years and is attended by thousands of Pathfinders and youth leaders from around the world. It was an honor to be asked, especially since I had fond memories of my own days as a Pathfinder.

It was a high-profile position that would demand a lot of my time and require some travel for board meetings and promotion of the event. As it turned out, the travel sometimes lasted several days, requiring me to be away from Christina and Madison longer than I wanted. It also created an intense spiritual battle since I often stayed in hotel rooms alone. I would toss and turn well into the night, attempting to resist the temptation to channel surf for racy television shows or movies. Eventually I would give in, rationalizing that the only way that I was going to get any sleep was to simply act out with something on TV. At times I was tempted to just purchase the adult movies that were offered through the hotel, but I realized that it would show up on my receipts that I would have to turn in on my expense report.

Anyone who has struggled with pornography will tell you that hotel rooms are a major trigger. There is an overwhelming sense of freedom and anonymity that is incredibly intoxicating. I didn't indulge every time I traveled, but the intensity of the spiritual struggle was at times too much to bear.

Next I was asked to serve as the cohost of a globally televised evangelistic outreach called Net '98. It would be broadcast directly from the campus of Andrews University[5] and feature the college church pastor, Dwight Nelson, as the speaker. I'm often asked how I was picked to participate in such a major denominational endeavor, and my reply is "I was a last resort!" I naively accepted the opportunity, not realizing that every night for more than 20 nights I would appear on a worldwide broadcast along with my cohost, Shasta. The scope of what we were doing didn't fully dawn on me until we started receiving faxes and e-mail messages from every corner of the globe.

My participation in that series gave me instant recognition on campus and around the country within the Adventist denomination. It became common for Shasta and me to hang around after the program signing autographs and taking pictures with people. I don't think either of us anticipated that type of response—after all, it was an evangelistic series! Even years later people often recognize me as "the guy from Net '98."

In spite of my apparent success, I was still hounded by an ongoing struggle with pornography. A part of me hoped that the Internet connection that I had through the university would have filters that would force me to keep clean while online, but that wasn't the case. I accessed porn regularly, often staying up late to study, only to stray off onto a porn site after Christina went off to bed. I discovered a virtual Disneyland of pornography, and it was during my time at the seminary that an addiction to Internet pornography began to take root, dragging me toward a five-year enslavement.

This poem, written by Pastor Daniel Henderson in his book *Think Before You Look,* describes so well the constant turmoil of longing to be free yet continuing to give in to sexual temptation.

A Lonely Lust*

A man sits alone with a choice before his eyes;
No one else is present as he wrestles with these lies.

BREAKING THE SILENCE

A fire smolders once again from deep within his soul;
He can fuel its growing heat or choose to leave it cold.

Passion begins to flow with a force against his will;
Scenes that grip his mind bring the promise of a thrill.
Emotions rage, needs unfold from a weak and lonely heart;
In this very private moment, will he stop or let it start?

A lovely wife, terrific kids have blessed his simple life;
His gracious God and prayerful friends stand by him in the strife.
But out of sight is out of mind in this moment of clear choice;
Even the indwelling Spirit speaks with ever-fading voice.

Images entice his spirit as their beauty pierce his reason;
Setting aside real joy and peace, he indulges for just a season.
More brief and empty now seems the thrill once it is done;
Regret and shame overwhelm as the lies again have won.

He walks away so dirty, feeling lost in his defeat;
Everything he really loves he chose again to cheat.
Full of remorse in this return to the filth of where he's been;
If only he knew how to stop this madness, before it starts again.

—Daniel Henderson

[1] A Seventh-day Adventist private day and boarding school for high school students
[2] The leader for campus spiritual activities.
[3] Pathfinders is a coed SDA youth organization similar to the Girl Scouts and Boy Scouts. Generally groups meet weekly for activities.
[4] Derived from "camp" plus "jamboree," this is a large gathering of Pathfinders for camping, social and physical activities, and spiritual nurture.
[5] This Adventist university is the home of the theological seminary for the SDA Church.

BREAKTHROUGH

"This, in essence, is the message we heard from Christ and are passing on to you: God is light, pure light; there's not a trace of darkness in him. If we claim that we experience a shared life with him and continue to stumble around in the dark, we're obviously lying through our teeth—we're not living what we claim. But if we walk in the light, God himself being the light, we also experience a shared life with one another, as the sacrificed blood of Jesus, God's Son, purges all our sin."—1 John 1:5-7, Message.

We returned to the Dallas–Fort Worth area in December 1999 at the height of the Y2K frenzy. We were eager to return to ministry life, settle down, and purchase a home. Shortly before we left the seminary, Christina gave birth to our second daughter, Brooklyn. Brooklyn's entrance into the world was complicated by a Group B strep infection unknowingly passed along to her by Christina. Prior to going into labor, Christina complained of headaches and for several days ran an unusually high fever. She felt that something was wrong, but her doctors never picked up on anything until it was too late. Right away the nurses noticed that Brooklyn was discolored and laboring to breathe. They allowed Christina only a few moments to hold her before they rushed her to the neonatal intensive-care unit. It was a scary time for us, since we weren't sure how much damage the infection had done. We spent the next couple weeks driving back and forth between home and the hospital to hold and feed

Brooklyn. Her health improved, and we were finally able to bring her home.

Back in Texas, I was fortunate enough to return to the same church I had served prior to leaving for the seminary. This time I would serve as an associate pastor, focusing my ministry on evangelism, preaching, and special projects. It was good to return to a familiar place. It was also good to return having by all appearances experienced some success while away at seminary. The church welcomed Christina and me back with open arms. During this time of transition my appetite for porn seemed to diminish. I was helped by the fact that we stayed in the home of church members during our search for a house, and there was hardly ever a time I was alone. Sensing that I was at a reprieve, I focused my energy on studying and working out. I saw our return to working with a local church as an opportunity for a fresh start and hoped that I could leave porn behind forever.

In February 2000 we purchased our first home. It was a terrific house and literally a godsend. For several weeks we had come up empty. Then out of nowhere, as we were driving in a neighborhood not far from the church, we noticed an older man standing in his front yard. He was pointing to his "For Sale by Owner" sign and grinning from ear to ear. We immediately pulled into the driveway and went in for an unscheduled viewing. The house was immaculately kept. It was smoke-free and had a sizable backyard just perfect for our growing family. We fell in love with it, and a couple days later returned with an offer. I could tell that Christina was very happy, especially since we'd spent our last months at the seminary in cramped student housing.

What I was unaware of was that during those years in Michigan, Christina became suspicious of my activity. But a couple years would pass before she told me that she was almost certain I was having an affair. She was partly right. She was tipped off one night when she got up and discovered me at the computer. Sometime during my evening of studying I detoured off into the world of erotica. Engrossed in what I was seeing, I was caught off guard when I heard Christina ask a probing question from the doorway: "What are you doing?"

I quickly clicked off the porn page and adjusted my posture, relieved that the monitor was positioned in such a way that it would have been difficult for her to see what was on the screen. However, Christina was no fool. Judging by my reaction to hearing her voice, she sensed that I was covering something up. Christina never said anything and made her way back into our bedroom, but I had a sick feeling that she knew what was going on. At that point a part of me desperately wanted to reach out to her and confess my long-held secret. Even then I realized that secrecy was likely the culprit keeping me enslaved. But I didn't confess that night, and the next morning in an awkward attempt to apologize for my unusual behavior I printed off a copy of the vows I read to her on our wedding day and left them at her bedside. She seemed bewildered and turned off by my gesture, and we never discussed what had happened the previous night.

Now we settled into our new home and reestablished relationships with church members and longtime friends while Christina embraced full-time stay-at-home motherhood with our girls. I attempted to settle back into ministry at the Arlington church, but sensed that it was time for me to take on my own congregation as senior pastor. Knowing that a seasoned minister had mentored me, I felt comfortable stepping into the role. I also had confidence in my own dreams and passions for ministry and was confident that I could make a significant impact in a church of my own.

In 2002 I got my opportunity to move into a senior pastor role. I was asked to serve in a two-church district on the south side of Dallas. This was the perfect opportunity, and it wouldn't require us to move. They were both very small congregations, with no more than 75 to 80 active attendees between the two churches. But I was excited to begin a new phase of my ministry, and the members of both churches seemed ecstatic that a young energetic couple had agreed to come lead their churches. By this time Christina was pregnant with our third daughter, Liberty.

We'd not planned on having any more children, and with Madison and Brooklyn getting older, Christina had hoped to resume her work on a college degree. This would delay her plans for some time.

Our house had a small building out back that the previous owner had used as a workshop. During our initial walk-through I eyed it as a possible home office and study, and with two active children in the house the workshop provided a good place for early-morning quiet time, study, and prayer. Not long after moving in, I decided that we should have a phone line installed so that I could answer the phone when I was out there and have access to the Web for sermon resources. Naively I assumed that while I would be tempted to look at porn, I could resist because of my new determination to quit. We purchased a family computer for the living room, but we also held on to an older computer that I kept out in my new study. And now that I had Internet access in a secluded location, the battle with porn came back with a vengeance.

This time my appetite for porn emerged stronger and more aggressive than I had remembered, and our newer, faster computer located prominently in our living room became a constant source of temptation when I was left alone. My renewed dependency on porn grew to the point that if Christina left the house to run an errand or pick up our girls from school, leaving me home alone, I couldn't resist going online. Careful to listen for the garage door or any sign that she and the girls had returned from an outing, I returned to adult sites I had frequented in the past. I'm not certain how long this went on, but apparently it reached a point at which I wasn't very good at covering my tracks. In the past I'd always been careful to erase the history and remove all the explicit images from the computer's cache. It had become increasingly more difficult to do this, however, since every time I looked at a porn site I was bombarded by pop-up ads. Still, I thought I was keeping my porn habit concealed from my wife.

I was the one being fooled. Christina had discovered something on the computer but needed time to build up enough courage to ask me if I had anything to do with it. Finally one evening as we were getting into bed, she informed me that she had been shocked to find raunchy images on our computer. Then she point-blank asked if I had been looking at porn. I was speechless. My heart pounded, my eyes grew wide, and my throat became dry and tight. I dropped my head in shame and with tears in my eyes acknowledged that indeed this had been a longtime battle for me.

Christina tearfully embraced me and assured me that she loved me in spite of my failing. It was at this time that she acknowledged the suspicions she'd had back when we were at the seminary, citing the late-night episode a couple years before. She agreed to support me and help me deal with the problem, but she also insisted that I be truthful with her and not hide from her what was going on. After we talked for a bit, I felt relieved that she now knew my secret. I felt that this was the breakthrough that God was really after with me—that there was now a crack in the vicelike grip that porn had on me. I was comforted by the fact that Christina said she wouldn't tell anyone, and I hoped that I would be able to keep my end of the bargain of staying away from porn. While there was a tremendous sense of relief after Christina and I talked, I still knew that I had a weakness for porn. Things did seem to subside for a bit, but I was faced with a new challenge when I moved into the pastor's study at my new church.

Ever conscious of my vulnerability to porn, I initially resisted having Internet access from my church study. After a few months, however, I started connecting through my personal dial-up account. Internally I justified having access to the Web because I used it to write e-mails to members, search for sermon illustrations, and do other research for upcoming messages. The church was small enough that I was there alone most of the day, with only the occasional interruption from a member dropping by to talk or the church janitor stopping in to clean. The church didn't supply me with a computer, so every day I carried my personal laptop to my study. This provided an easy way for me to keep my Internet activity concealed, since I was the only one using my laptop. Perhaps I had even convinced myself that since I wasn't using a church computer, I wasn't really hurting anything.

Now that I had a way to consistently feed my hunger for porn, I was often eager to get to my study, knowing that I would have time alone and the freedom to look at porn with little or no interruption. There were times I went to the office determined not to look at porn but would find myself online typing in vulgar key words. A big part of me felt ashamed that I was in the church indulging in something so vile. I wanted to resist—I longed to stop doing it. After one of my forays at the office, I even called a national Christian ministry because I felt desperate for someone to talk to about my problem. I spent some time on the phone with this ministry and signed up to receive information on a program that was successful at helping men overcome the addiction.

I knew that Christina had to be aware of my office escapades, having caught me at home a few times since my previous admission. But like an animal caught in a crude trap, scrambling to get free only to become more entangled, I was deeply entangled in pornography. Any effort I made to break free only strengthened porn's grip.

My occasional lapses with porn during my early ministry had now become a frequent and compulsive series of escapades on the Internet. I knew that things were out of control, but what could I do? The answer to that question had always lingered in my mind. I knew that I had to tell someone, but whom? Should I go to my local conference administrators? If I did that, how would my churches respond? Would I be fired? How would I support my family if I were terminated? What would people think of me? Having been around the church since my teenage years, I knew that there was low tolerance for such behavior.

With my secret forays onto the Web from my home computer, coupled with the escalating pattern of acting out that I had fallen into at my church office, things really went south during the summer of 2003. That's when Christina and the girls left for a week to attend one of our church's annual camp meetings, this one in Arizona.[*] I dreaded that time of the year, since I knew that I would be home alone in the evenings. In previous years during their trip, I hadn't fared very well. I could usually do OK for the first day or so, using sheer willpower to stay clean, but eventually I would wear down and give in, renting a racy video or surfing the Web well past midnight. This generally pushed me into a cycle of bingeing that lasted for days. When I would finally emerge from the haze of indulgence, I would get down on my knees and pray for God's forgiveness.

At my previous church during the summers, I directed a day camp program, and after camp I was at home alone. My new church didn't run the same program, so I kept my normal routine of working at my church office during the day and returning home in the evening. It should have been a time to rest and recuperate from the day's activities, but for me it turned into a time of anguish and despair.

Sure enough, after a day or so of white-knuckling it, I went online one evening after returning from the church. I told myself that I was going to hop online only long enough to check my e-mail and catch up on the day's news, but I wound up straying onto adult sites. I felt utterly defeated and miserable. I couldn't understand why I couldn't get past this thing. I sat in a daze staring out the window, feeling as though I was at the end of my rope. This was the bottom for me. I thought about how many years I had been on this roller coaster and how I so wanted to be free. *Something has to change, Bernie,* I told myself.

The little crack created from my disclosure to Christina broke open further when in my turmoil I looked to God, hoping that once and for all He would take this thing from me. In those moments God revealed to me something that He had quietly whispered to me all along: *I needed to tell someone.* In my own words I needed to confess to another human being the dark secret I held. I knew of only one person I trusted enough to unload my burden on—Mike. I knew that the senior pastor I had trained under and heard preach on grace so many times would be willing to listen to me.

Over the years I had seen Mike minister to people in the most desperate of situations, and now I was the one in need. But I was still deeply distraught over the thought of someone else knowing. I didn't like the thought of disappointing anyone else with my revelation. Agonizing over what to do, I held on to the phone for quite some time before finally getting up enough courage to call. Mike often counseled people at his church office, so fearing that someone might see me having a private session with him, I asked him to come to my house.

Mike arrived a short while later. We chatted for a few moments about ministry, and then I confessed to him how pornography had dogged my soul for years and had been a constant source of failure for me.

His response surprised me. "Join the club," he said. Mike calmly confirmed that in his ministry he had heard the same story from many men. He assured me that I wasn't alone in my struggle. He also asserted that pornography was not God's ideal for me. I shared a little more about what had transpired over the years and how I had been on a big-time binge the past couple days. Mike talked to me about praying a prayer of surrender of my sexuality to God, and before he left he led me in that prayer. In addition, I agreed to be in an accountability relationship with him during the coming months.

Something enormous happened to me on that day—I tasted freedom. For the first time as an adult, I knew that I would no longer be saddled with this sin. Those chains that had held me in bondage for so long were now beginning to break. I wasn't completely changed at once. It would be a couple more days before my wife and daughters returned home, and I again looked at porn during that time. But I knew that God was shattering porn's hold on me, and things were going to be different. For our family's sake, they had to be!

Christina later told me that before going on her trip she had reached an important decision. She had had enough. She had planned to separate from me if I hadn't shown some real progress by the time she returned. For her own sanity she felt that she needed to get away and let me deal with the issue alone. By God's grace, when she returned home, she found a different man.

★ This traditional Christian gathering is still an annual event for many Seventh-day Adventists.

Chapter 4

TURNING THINGS AROUND

"For I know the thoughts that I think toward you, says the Lord, thoughts of peace and not of evil, to give you a future and a hope."—Jeremiah 29:11.

No apologies
For who I'm meant to be
The only thing that matters is
I am free
When I am overwhelmed
Holding pieces of my heart
When I feel my world
Start to fall apart

To the cross I run
Holding high my chains undone
Now I am finally free
Free to be what I've become
Undone

Even in defeat
The face of tragedy
Still you'd have to say that
I found victory

In brokenness comes beauty
Divine fragility
Reminding me of nail-scarred hands
Reaching out for me.
—*MercyMe, "Undone"**

---

*T*hings were different now, and I didn't feel any pull to return to my old ways. I felt as though I had a new life, as if I were resurrected from the dead. Porn had ravaged my life for so long—to finally have a life without it was euphoric. God had finally gotten my attention on this issue, and now I wanted to live the life that I knew He always wanted for me. A life of freedom and joy, not the double life I had created. I didn't know much about "recovery" at the time, but I knew that I had to do something to regain what I had lost. There was no sense of triumphalism in me—or grand illusions that I would never have to worry about the temptation of pornography again. Instead, I felt a calm resolve and confidence that the Holy Spirit was truly working, now that I had allowed myself to become vulnerable to His leading.

The best way to describe it is an overwhelming sense of peace. In the same way that Jesus had spoken words and calmed the raging storm on the Sea of Galilee, He had brought peace to my soul. No more panicky feeling that someone would discover my sin, no more hiding or scrambling to cover up my activity, no more anxious feelings when left alone. Just peace. As a result, my prayer and devotional life took on a different tone. With the anxiety over my ongoing battle with pornography removed, I spent less time begging for God's mercy and more time genuinely embracing the God I knew had delivered me. I began to seek depth and substance over the shallow and cheap quick fix of porn. The pace of my mornings slowed so that I could take in more of God at home, surrounded by my family, rather than racing off to my church office. I realized that my life was becoming whole again.

At the same time, I was also very much aware of how short-lived victory could be. God had won a great battle for me, but the war still raged on all around. Knowing that the enemy would intensify his efforts in light of my recent conversion meant that I had to better equip myself. Since the Internet had been my drug of choice, I decided that I couldn't use any Internet connection outside of our home. I stuck to a pledge I made to Christina that I would spend less time on the Internet altogether and wouldn't access the Internet from anywhere but home—and only when she was there.

I also began reading everything I could find about sexual addiction—pornography addiction, in particular. I thought it would be wise to become educated on the issue in order to fight a more effective battle. I read articles and books, listened to sermons, and studied whatever else I could find on the topic, both from Christian and secular experts. One of the most important books I read during this time was *Every Man's Battle*. I had heard of the book somewhere along the way and even thought of purchasing it at one point during my own crisis, but because of the title I was always afraid of what the cashier would think when I was checking out. That wasn't an issue anymore, so right away I went and bought the book. Once I opened it, I couldn't put it down. It was as if the authors had followed me around my entire life, journaling my up and down journey with porn. There are so many experiences in the book that resembled my own. I was moved by the authors' transparency and honesty as they recounted their own stories of sexual sin and failure. It was a very revealing book and helped to boost my own resolve to live a life of purity.

Every Man's Battle also helped to answer that nagging, somewhat naive question I had always had: Was I the only Christian man (pastor) who struggled in this area? The answer was a resounding no! The book's title aptly describes the reality of our situation as men, because truly, this is *every* man's battle. Now for the first time I began to realize that there was a way for men to fight back and win. *Every Man's Battle* was full of Bible passages that I had read many times before but now seemed to pack much more punch. I devoured the book in just a couple days, making notes in the margins and highlighting and underlining many of the key points and teachings.

Perhaps the most important part of the book was the honest and open approach the authors took as they addressed the issue from a Christian perspective. To have the authors reveal such deeply personal information about their journey as Christian men impacted me profoundly. In reality I longed for the same honesty and authenticity that I read in that book. Over the years I had bought into the protocol of most church cultures—pretending and masquerading as something you aren't in order to avoid conflict. And you could certainly never let anyone know that you had a sin problem. In most church cultures vulnerability is indirectly discouraged due to the disruption and discomfort it has the potential to cause. I found *Every Man's Battle* surprisingly refreshing, for it revealed that Christians do have struggles, even struggles that are distasteful to talk about. I had a deep desire to reflect that type of authenticity and honesty on this issue within the context of my own denomination.

Then, too, the book whetted my appetite for more significant recovery work. I thought about the obvious option of finding a Christian counselor or therapist but really wanted a different experience—something that was more potent in the immediate sense. I knew about the Every Man's Battle (EMB) multiday workshop that a national ministry called New Life Ministries sponsored around the country once a month (at that time). One of the book's authors, Stephen Arterburn, is the founder of New Life Ministries. I remembered that several months back, after a binge in my church study, I had even called New Life to ask about the program and what it involved. At the time that I called I wasn't ready to receive any serious help, so I never followed up.

I wasn't certain that the EMB workshop was the thing for me. It was expensive and would require that I be away for several days. (The workshop is shorter and less expensive now.) I didn't want to go if it would just be a good, heartwarming experience but lack the substantive biblical teaching as well as clinical support I was looking for in order to remain pure. But I decided that if the workshop was anything like the book, then it was exactly what I wanted and needed.

As it turned out, the conference was scheduled to be in Dallas in October—just a few months after my living-room confession to Mike—and I determined that I wouldn't let anything keep me from attending that workshop. There is a track specifically designed for pastors and other church leaders to receive training on how to deal with the issue among men in their churches. For a moment I thought that maybe this would be a good way for me to attend without letting anyone in on my own issues with porn. But I knew that I needed this conference for myself. While I could have easily attended under the guise of a church leader, I had to admit that I, the caregiver, now needed care.

I decided to approach my congregations and request some financial support to attend the upcoming "pastors' conference." At the time, the church was unaware of my problem, and I wasn't ready to bring them in until I received some outside help first. Because of some other issues going on in the church, my request initially received a cool reception in the board meeting. I never pressed the issue, and even though the board ultimately voted to approve the funding, I chose not to use the church's funds.

Using the professional allowance I'm given as a pastor every year and our own personal savings, I pulled together enough money to attend the October conference. I couldn't help being excited, almost giddy, with anticipation about attending. I felt God working and knew that this would be one more way He would continue to break the hold of porn in my life. My confirmation letter and information packet arrived a few weeks prior to the conference. It described the format of the workshop and outlined the guidelines for anyone in attendance. Because of the sensitive nature of the topic, great care was taken to ensure the privacy of each attendee.

I was basking in my newfound freedom, and I hoped that this would be a place that I could talk about it. I wasn't disappointed. Close to 80 men packed into a small conference room of the hotel where the workshop was being held. I walked in a few minutes before the meeting started and scanned the seats for a place to sit. I almost expected to see a familiar face and was somewhat relieved that everyone was a stranger. It allowed me the freedom to take in the conference without having to do any explaining. I don't know if it was visible to anyone else, but underneath my straight demeanor I was bursting with joy and had to work to keep a smile off my face.

The opening session was on a Wednesday night, and after a time of praise and worship, the workshop facilitator, Joe Dallas, began by sharing his own story of sexual addiction and recovery. I sat completely engaged in his talk, amazed at how easily he could share such deep personal information. Joe's talk wasn't pretty. Exposed to pornography at age 8, Joe was seduced and eventually molested by a man in a bathroom stall.[1] The molestation continued for years and even involved other men. As an adult, Joe eventually fell into group sex, homosexuality, and pornography.[2] After listening to Joe's story I felt like I needed to be in another workshop for those who hadn't strayed quite so far. Then I realized that there wasn't much difference between Joe's sin and mine; it was just a matter of activity. I was still guilty of the same sin—it just took a different form. Listening to Joe's story did open my eyes to just how far sexual addiction can go.

The teaching sessions involved filling in blanks in our workshop notebook as the PowerPoint presentation revealed the answers on the screen. Joe moved through each teaching session with depth and humor, projecting a tremendous sense of empathy toward each man in the room. There were boxes of tissues positioned at the end of each row of chairs—a clear indicator that this would be an emotionally draining experience. Each of us men would be impacted by the lessons in a different way as we recalled the way our activity had disrupted our lives and the lives of the ones we love.

I was amazed at how each session was incredibly quiet and somber, as though each man in the room was silently acknowledging the truths he heard. The silence was broken only by Joe's voice and the occasional sound of men weeping quietly. Right away it became very apparent to me that our team of facilitators knew what they were talking about and were serious about following the Bible's counsel on helping men find freedom. At the end of the teaching sessions, we could write any questions on 3" x 5" index cards and have the facilitators answer them in front of the entire group. Some of the questions got the entire group laughing, which broke some of the built-up tension. Other questions provoked more discussion and inquiries from the group. I found this time to be extremely beneficial and contributed several questions of my own throughout the conference.

The group sessions were the most powerful part of the workshop. All the participants were divided into smaller groups with a therapist as the group leader. The group leader's job was simply to allow each one of us to tell our sordid story in a reasonable amount of time and then listen to the other group members respond in an appropriate way. I had never been in a situation like this before. It felt like something out of a television show, and I had always been a little leery of such a format. But as each man began to volunteer his story, I couldn't help feeling an instant bond. Any reservations I had about "group" were totally gone. As I sat and listened to each man, I realized the common theme among all the men—they had never talked about their problem either.

My assigned roommate during the conference was a firefighter from a small city in east Texas. He was a sincere and devoted husband who had become sidetracked by phone sex and Internet pornography. As I sat in one of our group sessions and listened to his story, I couldn't hold back the tears when he told of his anguish over hurting his wife. There was no arrogance or pride; he had become teachable, moldable, broken. Not every man reaches that point. I have come across men who can't seem to grasp the depth of their sin, seeing it as a minor issue impacting only themselves.

To my shame, I had displayed a similar rebellious spirit after my wife had confronted me. Though I said that I would deal with the problem, I never took any concrete action to stop my destructive behavior. I was at the point that I find many men—they have a level of discomfort with the fact that pornography has such a level of control on their lives, but at the same time they enjoy the pleasure of their sin and refuse to embrace the level of discomfort required to be free.

I came away from the Every Man's Battle workshop knowing that God had done a powerful work in my heart. I can truly say that I have never known the camaraderie and fellowship that I experienced in those group sessions. We became a band of brothers who shared a common battle, and our battle stories bonded us together like nothing else. I wish I could say that I've remained in touch with those men, and for a brief while I did, but for the most part I have lost touch with all of them. But we will always be connected. I will always remember their stories and their tears. I do pray for them when they come to mind. I pray that they don't fall back into that old life.

The workshop required us to do some work once we got home to help us maintain sobriety: things such as establishing an accountability relationship, attending group meetings, and closely following the prescribed strategies outlined for us during the workshop. Another important step involved disclosing our secret activity to our wives in a more specific way. I gave myself a few days after the workshop to build up enough courage to look Christina in the eye and disclose to her all that I had been doing. The conference had prepared me to do this, but it still wasn't easy. Christina responded in her normal pleasant and gracious way, kissing me on the cheek and thanking me for opening up.

My guess is that she was somewhat hesitant to fully embrace my new walk until I could really earn her trust back by staying clean. But I could tell that she was happy about the noticeable change in me. In the past she had seen a man who was distant, as if he were off in a foreign land. A man who lacked contentment and peace and always seemed as though he needed more or something different. Now she saw a man opening up and sharing more of himself with her and the kids. I felt that I still had so much ground to make up. So much had been lost in the years that I had indulged in pornography. Time with the kids, intimate talks with

Christina, even meaningful friendships were cheated because of my preoccupation with pornography. But I was grateful for a second chance and a new beginning.

One of the concepts from the workshop that really hit home had to do with "converting" our wounds. The idea is to take a painful experience and transform it into something positive that will impact God's kingdom for good. From the moment I heard the facilitator speak about this, my mind was filled with thoughts of how God could turn the pain of my wound into something worthwhile. Since I knew that sexual sin festers in secrecy, I was impressed that I should begin to talk about this issue publicly. I wasn't sure how I would have an opportunity to speak out, considering the subject matter. But I was at peace to let God open the doors for me to share my story when the time was right.

---

[1] Joe Dallas, *The Game Plan*, p. xiv.
[2] *Ibid.*, p. xvi.

Chapter 5

My Story:
Devastation and Tragedy

by Christina Anderson

In fourth grade I attended a multigrade school, and in the spring the whole school played softball together. I remember the teacher positioning us; all of us smaller kids hoped to get on a team with one of the bigger kids. Michael was the biggest kid in our school, a tall, lean eighth-grader whom we all looked up to. To us he seemed invincible. But in one particular game Michael lost that invincibility. Michael was playing catcher as a first-grader came up to bat. She swung and the bat made contact with the ball. It was a foul popped up into the air, and Michael jumped up to catch it. This is the part I will never forget. As he stood up, she swung around with the bat, and it stopped when it hit Michael right in the stomach. Having no protective equipment, he came crashing down with a loud groan, all of us looking on in shock . . . invincible Michael.

It was a muggy Texas night, like most Texas summer evenings. I had just put our two girls to bed and decided to hop online to check my e-mail. I remember logging on and typing in that familiar www; then I stopped. For where Hotmail, MSNBC, or some other familiar address would normally be, I saw something that made me uneasy, that actually made me sick to my stomach. That something there staring at me in the address box . . . did I dare click on it? I did, hoping that it was not—could not—be what I thought that it was, but it took only a glance to confirm my fears. Of course, maybe it was a mistake or an accident. I scrambled to the history box. Scanning each day, closely looking over every little detail, confirmed that this was no mistake. There was pornography on my computer, viewed there over the past three days. Viewed while I was gone or asleep. I shut down the computer, then quickly turned it back on and erased those terrible files, hoping that it would erase the images in my mind and remove the aching feeling in my heart.

It took four days for me to get up the courage to confront Bernie about what I had found. I had just returned from a *Women of Spirit* conference with some friends and was feeling that God was nudging my heart. Bernie knows that whenever I say "We need to talk," it's serious. I really don't think that he knew that I had found him out yet. It felt as though the heaviness of my heart could be felt in the whole room as I told him about what I had found and seen. To my surprise, he didn't try to deny looking at Internet pornography. I had imagined he would try to get out of owning up. But what came next shocked me, shaking me to my core. For Bernie, my husband of seven years, told me that he had been struggling with a pornography problem for years. All I remember him saying is "for years," as in all the years we were dating, all the years we were married, the years our children were conceived, the 18 months I'd been pregnant . . . *the whole time.* All I could think was that our whole seven years of marriage had been tainted. Like a bat to the stomach, those words—the ones he said and the ones I heard—hit my heart, and I came crashing down, except that I did it inside where no one could see.

Naively I assumed that with his being confronted, with our talking about it, and with Bernie saying that he would change, he would blaze a new path. I, of course, knew nothing of the power of pornography addiction. I didn't even know that there was such a thing as porn *addiction*. Blindly I thought that with my love and support Bernie could beat this, but I was terribly, terribly wrong.

My life was filled with anxiety for the next two years as I easily saw signs that Bernie remained involved in pornography. Early-morning computer sessions, clicking off the computer when I walked in the room, spending less time at home and more time at the office, and disengaged phone conversations . . . I would try to monitor all this to figure out ways to make him stop, and it was making me crazy. He would go in cycles of repentance and a desire to be close to our family. Then there'd be a longing to pull away, to flee to his fantasy world. In retrospect that was our whole married life. I had seen this repeated time and time again but had no idea that an addiction to pornography was tied to it. He was close, and he was far away. Now I knew why. Each time he came back, I welcomed him. After all, I loved him. I adored him. But one day I realized that I was loving him at the cost of myself.

I grew up going to annual camp meetings in Arizona and decided to carry on the tradition with our girls. Every summer we headed down to Prescott to spend 10 days with their grandparents, taking in all the camp meeting activities. And it was during camp meeting that summer of 2003 that I cried out to God. I told Him that I was finished. That I had tried being the loving, forgiving, supportive wife, but that wasn't enough and I had to have some peace. I thought that maybe Bernie needed something to shock him, to show him that I was serious. I would not live like this anymore.

Thankfully, God was working on Bernie's heart just as I was gathering the strength to become a stronger person. When I returned home, I found something different. Something in Bernie had changed. Bernie had finally opened up to another person, his mentor and our dear friend, Mike Tucker. Bernie shared his struggle, and with love Mike helped give Bernie the push toward recovery that he needed. Hopeful, yet wary in what I saw, I decided that God had heard me and that He was telling me to stay. I watched and waited.

Being a pastor's family is ironic in some ways. Everyone knows you, but no one knows *you*. There is a certain professional distance you maintain. With an issue of sexual sin it is especially difficult. Up until Bernie opened up to Mike, no one but us knew of his struggle. I had spoken to no one. I couldn't even imagine what kind of problems this would cause for Bernie's ministry if I did. *I* could barely handle this—what would our family and friends think, let alone the conservative base of our church? So I kept silent. In fact, I hardly spoke to Bernie about it except when I felt that he needed to be confronted. Part of me was afraid that he would console himself with more porn and part of me was unable to verbalize what I felt. Looking back, I know this was the biggest mistake of my life. It was such a toxic way to live. However, I did find one safe place. In my room listening to music, I cried to God all my fears, all my hurts, and all my anger. Always there, waiting for me, was my heavenly Father.

Four months after he talked with Mike, Bernie attended an Every Man's Battle workshop. That conference—what he gained there, how God used it to change his life—is truly amazing. I saw a different person in Bernie after that conference. I remember that several days after he returned home, he sat me down to apologize to me. I was astonished at how heartfelt it was, but I was still apprehensive about trusting him completely. He, of course, was on fire. Bernie is like that. When he is passionate about something, he is 100 percent. Within a few months he was telling the conference administration about his addiction and talking about going public with his testimony. I, on the other hand, was trying to keep up with it all. It was moving too fast. First an addiction to pornography, then an advocate against pornography—all within four to five months! Ever supportive, I gave my blessing. My motive was tainted, however. I hoped that Bernie's being *against* pornography would keep him *away* from pornography.

Then on March 2, 2004, everything in my world spun out of control. On that date my younger brother, John, tragically died from a terrible accident. The next few weeks were the darkest of my life. My family was devastated. Bernie (who had gotten sick the week before the accident) was so ill that I was shuttling him back and forth to hospitals, and then I suddenly remembered that Bernie was going public with his testimony and we hadn't yet told our families or friends. At that point I should have stopped it all for my own sanity, for my own well-being, but I still was unable to say what I needed.

The following years brought their own struggles—trying to let go of the pain of the past, trying to rebuild trust, gradually becoming comfortable with Bernie openly talking about his addiction, and dealing with the grief of losing my brother. It helped that I had seen such a change in Bernie and a transformation of our marriage. And with some Christian counseling and God's guidance I learned and am learning to say what I need and how I feel. All these things are finally bringing the healing that I need. One of my favorite songs is by the Christian group Third Day. It's a song about how love can heal your heart even when you don't think it's possible. My favorite part is "When you think your life is shattered;/And there's no way to be fixed again;/ Love heals your heart;/At a time you least expected;/You're alive like you have never been;/Love heals your heart."*

Love has helped to heal my heart, and though the journey is far from over, I find myself thinking less of the past and more of today.

Since Bernie has been sharing his testimony I have been sadly surprised at the number of Christian couples that tell me they are living with the same issue. I have had some women ask me what they should do, where they should go. This journey is long and painful, but the end result is so very worth it. If someone had told me five years ago that Bernie would be the man he is today, I would not have believed it. Here are some of the things that I have learned that may be able to help you in your journey.

1. Find someone to confide in. My biggest mistake was keeping all my feelings bottled up. It only made the healing process much harder and longer than it needed to be. You need to find someone who is on your side and who is on the side of your marriage. It will not benefit you if your trusted friend can say only negative things about your husband and your marriage. A true friend will listen to you and give you a shoulder to cry on without having to always give her input.

2. Find a spiritual outlet. We all have different ways that we connect with God. For some, it is an early-morning devotional time, while others seek Him out in nature. Whatever way you are able to bring yourself to the feet of God, it is so important. For me, I have always been able to hear God most clearly in music and stillness. Allowing the words of the songs to penetrate my heart helped me find my way home so many times.

3. Acknowledge your wound. As a girl, I loved Wonder Woman. She could do anything, but Wonder Woman I am not. I am not sure why I have found it so difficult to verbalize to Bernie the depth of the pain that his choices caused me. Truth be told, I am quite sure that he'll never quite get it, for a woman's heart is a complicated thing. I do know that when I was able to begin to say the words, it freed a part of me to forgive, to forget, and to heal.

4. Show grace. I am constantly amazed at how cruelly people who "love" each other can treat their own spouses. In my life I have been shown such grace by the Father and have seen grace modeled throughout my childhood. When it was my turn, I chose to act with grace as well, showing compassion and love while holding Bernie accountable.

5. Don't look at *Cosmo*. I remember thinking again and again that I could never look like those women in the magazines. I'm a pretty simple girl, and I knew that there was no way for me to compete with that. But still I was constantly comparing myself to everyone I saw and wondering who Bernie would think was more attractive than I am. I was making myself sick, so I stopped looking. I stopped glancing at the magazine covers in the grocery store, stopped watching evening TV, and did whatever it took for as long as it took. It seems silly, but to always be comparing yourself with an airbrushed cover girl can really damage your self-esteem.

If you find yourself or your spouse in this battle, I pray that you find the inner strength and courage to fight for your marriage and for yourself. It is worth it. It is truly worth it.

---

*© 2005, Consuming Fire Music (admin.). All rights reserved.

Chapter 6

Absorbing the Blow

"I felt like my marriage was dying, and by the summer of 2003 I was fed up and thinking of separation, because I thought it might be the shock therapy that he needed to finally decide to delete the pornography from our lives."—Christina Anderson.[1]

"Blessed are those who mourn, for they will be comforted."—Matthew 5:4.

When your phone rings in the middle of the night, there's an instant gut-wrenching sense that something terrible has happened. On March 1, 2004, at around 11:30 p.m., Christina's mother called to tell us that Christina's younger and only brother, J.P., had been critically injured in an accident while working in her parents' garage. He was alive and stable but had suffered major head injuries, and was being flown to a nearby trauma center in Las Vegas.

Our stress levels were already at monumental levels, since this was shortly after my public confession. Church members and friends were reacting in all kinds of ways. Most were mainly concerned with Christina's well-being, some wanted to know the status of my employment, and some sought counsel for themselves. Christina was being bombarded with awkward questions about how she was dealing with things and having to listen to friends share their own stories about a spouse's missteps in the same area. Our marriage was stable, but obviously things were tenuous. Needless to say, this couldn't have come at a more difficult time.

To add to an already challenging situation, a few days earlier I had come down with a stomach virus that in previous weeks had made its way through Christina and our three kids. Since I have a history of colon problems, the virus triggered a major flare-up of ulcerative colitis. My health worsened, and so did the situation with Christina's brother, which held our main attention. I don't believe that Christina slept at all that night, and I caught a few winks between trips to the bathroom. Of course, we earnestly prayed for J.P., but early the next morning we received word from her dad that he had passed away during the night while in surgery.

This was, and still is, totally devastating to her family. Unlike my family, Christina's family has always been extremely close. I come from a situation of divorce, but her parents have been together for more than 25 years. Christina grew up in a small town, Topock, on the westernmost edge of Arizona, and her parents still live in the same house. The town is located in the Mojave Desert, which I often tease her about, referring to it as hell because of the extremely hot summertime temperatures.

Christina's family has always been tight-knit, spending time together on family vacations, backyard barbeques, and Sabbath afternoon jeep rides in the desert, along with endless summer boating trips to the nearby frigid Colorado River. They always say "I love you" when they get off the phone, and tears are shed when they must say goodbye in person. It's been somewhat of an adjustment for me. My family has always been rather distant, expressing affection at times but not overdoing it. When Christina and I were first married, I felt a little annoyed that every night she had to talk to her parents and that every family vacation seemed to include them.

With the public disclosure of my porn problem and the death of Christina's brother, this was the darkest time of our lives. It finally got the best of me the day Christina flew out to be with her family. The girls and I were scheduled to fly out the next day, and so much had to be done to get them ready for the trip. (If you've ever traveled with kids, you know what I mean.) I did my best to try to hold it together, but after dropping off the girls at a friend's house in order to run some errands kid-free, I was overcome with emotion. Breathing a deep sigh, I pulled over and wept aloud.

It was enough that I had caused my wife such pain through my sin, but now she was being hit again with the death of J.P. She grieved two losses: a tremendous loss of trust and faith in me for betraying her, and now the loss of her only brother. Upon arriving at her parents' home in Arizona, Christina quickly stepped in and took control of the situation. She didn't take much time to grieve herself, keeping busy with funeral arrangements, managing household business, and comforting everyone else. She would tell you that her relationship with God grew somewhat cold during this time, as it often does for people who have suffered a great loss. I've heard her say more than once that she was angry at God and not on speaking terms with Him. Here's how she describes it in her own words: "I was not speaking to Him, but when I was ready to listen, He taught me something very important. He said to me, 'Christina, you have to love Me for who I am, not for what I do.'" Yet even in the midst of her grief and anguish with God, she demonstrated incredible grace, patience, and endurance.

The most difficult part was that I couldn't do much to help her. I had hoped to be well enough to officiate at the funeral and then check into the hospital. But my health deteriorated further, and I ended up in the hospital earlier than planned, missing the funeral and any opportunity to support Christina and her family. The time in the hospital meant hours of just lying around. Between nursing assessments and doctor visits, I had an opportunity to quietly think about what was going on. I never questioned what God was doing along the way. Even in our pain I knew that God was with us. But like anybody, I just wanted everything to end. I wanted relief for Christina, if nothing else. I remember lying in the hospital bed asking God again and again, "Why?" Why had this happened? Why couldn't I be there for Christina? She had always been there for me.

Christina is innocent, faithful, and pure. She has a heart of compassion for children especially. Her Sabbath school class is the most popular gathering in our church. Unlike me, she's shy and reserved and takes a bit to warm up to strangers—which provides a good balance for her extroverted, outgoing husband! My wife isn't perfect. At times she exhibits evidence of her fallen nature, just like the rest of us. I also know that she grows weary at times of ministry life, probably wishing I had chosen a different line of employment. Yet she moves about with patience and kindness, submitting to the unpredictable nature of my schedule and often enduring extended periods of single motherhood. And her life hasn't been free of the messiness that comes with existing in this sinful world.

She was born to a teenage mother who had been taken advantage of by an older man who quickly exited the scene upon hearing of the pregnancy. Her birth father even lived in the same area throughout Christina's childhood, yet to this day he has never made an attempt to become involved in her life. I can't help thinking that a lingering sense of abandonment haunts Christina even as an adult. Thankfully, God provided a real man to step in and take her as his own daughter, providing a loving, secure, and stable environment.

Christina's parents stumbled upon the Adventist Church while Christina was in grade school. They, like so many others, initially took a fairly hard-core approach to their newfound faith. Becoming a vegetarian and giving up Saturday morning cartoons were a bit of a shock for Christina and her brother. Her parents also enrolled them in the small Adventist school housed in the local church building. Even prior to joining the Adventist Church, her parents understood the ways of the world and sought to protect Christina's innocence. She didn't go to a mall until she was a teenager, and she never saw a movie until she was well into her teens. Her parents were right, of course, to attempt to shield her from the murky realities of this world, but once you grow into adulthood, it's inevitable that you'll encounter the harshness of life in a fallen world.

When my wife learned about my sexual addiction, she described her devastation in an article written by Loretta Parker Spivey:

"I felt betrayed. It was as if I did not know the man I had been married to for seven years. I questioned our relationship and my entire marriage up to that point.

"I felt inadequate. Why would my husband have to look at women in books or on a computer screen? What was wrong with me?

"I felt alone. My husband was a pastor. Although I was angry, and hurt, I wanted to protect him. I never told a soul. Not my best friend, not my parents, not anyone. It is hard to carry another person's burden—hide another person's secret. It's really hard."

"This thing really affects your self-esteem, and self-image. It tore me down to my core. I felt like I am not good enough."[2]

The feelings of betrayal, inadequacy, and loneliness blend together like the ingredients of a crude, unstable bomb, placing a woman, especially, in a volatile, desperate state of mind. Often a woman will go for years living this way, refusing to leave her husband out of fear or uncertainty about how she and her children would survive without a provider. Other women fall into the role of therapist, becoming obsessed with fixing their husbands, ultimately neglecting their own spiritual and emotional health. I don't want to travel too far down this path about a woman's pain—since I'm not a woman. It's like announcing the birth of a child and the father saying, "It was really hard." I don't feel I have the right, especially as one who has caused such grief and pain. But this is a chapter about my wife and her journey through this, so I do want you to hear her voice and to some extent understand her pain and grief. There are many Christian women suffering through similar experiences right now. Perhaps just to acknowledge your pain and validate your journey provides some comfort.

More important, we urge women to seek out real help as well. The natural tendency of a wife is to protect, nurture, and guide her family at the expense of her own health. But this problem is too big! There will have to be a supporting cast to help guide you through. You will have to talk to someone. The relief of having gotten it off of your chest will soothe the embarrassment of letting someone know about the problem. Often the irony is that a woman feels less than faithful for exposing her husband's sin. She suffers in silence, praying that one day he'll wake up fixed. Or she'll fall into the trap of trying to become sexier, going out and spending money on lingerie—even being willing to accommodate her husband's tainted sexual adventures.

For the husbands, I hope you'll hear the message of my story, which is the message of this book: breaking the silence on your secret lust problem is the only way to find freedom. Your freedom has broader implications than you might realize. Much hinges on your coming clean and getting a handle on things now. Think of your children. They should motivate you toward getting clean and staying clean. Imagine the horror and trauma of one of your little ones discovering your secret porn stash or accidentally walking in on you in the very act! Heaven forbid your little boy carries on the legacy of lust because of his father's refusal to take a stand. The question I've asked myself time and again is the question you have to ask yourself: How do you want your children, your wife, and your church to see you? Do you want them to honor you, admire you, and respect you? The good news is that the research is actually on your side. Marriage and family therapist Dr. Jill Manning, who has conducted research on this subject, has found that in 87 percent of the cases where the husband confessed a problem with pornography, the marriages remained intact.[3]

But your wife is enduring a torment that you will never know. A woman's heart, her very identity, is rocked by the discovery of your secret sin. For you to continue in it, even after she knows, only does further damage. If for no other reason than to relieve your wife of the hell she's enduring, you should seek out help. Christina's comments provide a proper perspective: "People, especially Christians, need to know that pornography *is* a big deal. It's not just looking at a few pictures. It changes everything and has a long-lasting, negative impact on both the spouses and the marriage relationship."[4]

For the wives, you have to remember that you can't force your husband to deal with his porn problem. You can certainly turn up the heat, which I readily endorse. A man needs to experience the consequences of his sin. But you don't help things by making the appointment with the therapist for him or by forcing him to attend a group meeting. In some ways doing this only encourages his passivity about the problem. Christina apparently realized this in dealing with me: "There were two very l-o-n-g years from the time I found out about Bernie's addiction to the time he got serious about getting help. No matter how much I wanted to, I could not make the decision for him. He had to decide he wanted to do something different because it's not about having the willpower to stay away from pornography and sexual sin in all of its forms; it's about letting God transform a life."[5]

Let me add here that it isn't just his problem, either. Indirectly it is your problem, too, since you vowed before God and witnesses that you would remain faithful "in sickness and in health." This has to include spiritual sickness as well as physical ailment. In other words, to marry is to invite a level of disorder to our lives. The problem, while primarily experienced by one, does not exclude the other from involvement in the process of recovery.

I know that Christina sees this thing as I do—as all-out spiritual warfare with an enemy hell-bent on destroying marriages. Christina called me when I was traveling back from an interview at Focus on the Family. She told me how she had listened to another interview with Dr. Dobson that very day in which he talked about coming under intense spiritual attack as he served on a presidential commission studying the detrimental impact of pornography on society. Dr. Dobson apparently described how he felt that his life was in danger—and how both his son and daughter were almost killed during the time he served on the commission.

I had the same conversation with him in the studio during a break in the interview. When I told him of my brother-in-law's death and the illnesses we had endured, he related to me the same experience Christina had heard on the radio. Christina felt that that's exactly what was happening to us—that because I (we) were fighting back and taking a stand against pornography, the enemy set his sights on discouraging us from moving out together united in faith. It isn't easy for a husband and wife to come back from this stuff. A woman's heart doesn't heal overnight, and her anger won't subside in a day. Satan will use fear and discouragement to dissuade couples from diving in and making a change. The enemy will come after you relentlessly.

If you're a guy on the path toward recovery now, don't be surprised that your wife is further behind than you are. Don't be surprised if your euphoria over experiencing some freedom isn't shared by your spouse. Her wounds need time to heal. My wife describes her experience in relating to my newfound freedom in this way: "Here is where I struggle. I came into the process about 20 years after his first exposure to pornography. So it feels as if I have some catching up to do. While he has crossed the bridge, it feels like I am still on the bridge, and it's an unsteady, swinging bridge that threatens to dump me into the all-consuming, frigid, raging waters below."[6]

The healing continues for us years later. I can't get those lost years back that were wasted with porn. But God does offer a promise in the book of Joel: "I will repay you for the years the locusts have eaten—the great locust and the young locust, the other locusts and the locust swarm—my great army that I sent among you" (Joel 2:25). What I can do is embrace the life that I now know, looking ahead together with Christina and our girls. Christina is still making her way across the bridge, but I believe that she has picked up the pace. I can't blame her for taking her time when she's been wounded deeply. I do know that I'll be there when she gets to the other side, with arms outstretched ready to join her on the journey ahead.

---

[1] Loretta Parker Spivey, "The Bridge to Freedom," *Message*, July/August 2004, p. 19.

[2] *Ibid.*

[3] Jill Manning, L.P.C., "A Qualitative Study of the Supports Women Find Most Beneficial When Dealing With a Spouse's Sexually Addictive or Compulsive Behaviours" (docoral study), p. 69.

[4] Spivey, p. 23.

[5] *Ibid.*

[6] *Ibid.*

GOING PUBLIC

"He who conceals his sins does not prosper, but whoever confesses and renounces them finds mercy."—Proverbs 28:13.

Where a man's wound is that is where his genius will be.
Where his wounds lie there he finds his gift to the community.—Robert Bly.

In November 2003 I walked into my conference president's office to share my story. My ministerial director joined us. When I had finished, the president was rather shocked at the revelation and seemed even more taken aback when I shared with him that, according to a *Leadership* article, nearly 40 percent of pastors are struggling with pornography.* That meant that at least 40 or more of the 100 or so pastors expected to attend the upcoming pastors' meetings could possibly be struggling. I asked him if I could share my story with the group as a way to approach the topic and offer support to others who might be in trouble. He agreed without hesitation. For me, it was affirmation of what God was doing in my life.

I worked on the finishing touches for the talk while sitting in the lobby of the hotel where we were meeting. Other pastors mingled and talked in little groups around the lobby and dining area. I wondered if somehow word had gotten out that I would be talking about pornography.

It's difficult to describe my feelings that day, but I'll

never forget them. There was a holy exhilaration and a reverence and awe that I have never known before. I was about to be laid bare and vulnerable; all the pretense and masks would be off. This is what freedom felt like, and it was hard to contain my emotions. I felt naked and unashamed as I spent that last hour or so before my talk, writing down exactly what I was going to say.

I was almost in tears before I ever stood up to speak as I felt the presence of the Spirit of God. The long-held secret was now coming to light in a big way, and little did I know that that which I was so afraid of before would be the beginning of a story that God would use to heal and encourage many others.

More than 100 pastors and their spouses were present at this mandatory retreat. I shared with them my story of first being exposed to pornography at the age of 9. I told them about my acting out with pornography while serving as a pastor and how porn and lust had been a longtime struggle for me. My eyes welled with tears when I talked about my wife supporting me through all of this.

At the end of my talk, some of the group stood and applauded with tears running down their faces. Some voiced a strong "amen." Others remained quiet and seated. One of the conference officials got up to speak after me and remarked that in all of his years in ministry, he had never experienced anything like this at a pastors' meeting.

The group was told to keep my talk in confidence, which I knew was a bit of a joke considering how church people talk. Sure enough, it wasn't but a few days later that one of the pastors at that retreat told his congregation my story. He apologized to the conference and to me, but I wasn't hurt by what he had done. I felt that it was a story that needed to be heard, and sure enough, this was the beginning of many more opportunities.

The Media

On Valentine's Day 2004 a Dallas billboard read: "Her gift for Valentine's? Stop looking at porn." The billboard was the brainstorm of a Dallas-based ministry called NetAccountability.

NetAccountability is software designed to keep a log of a person's Internet activity and then send it to a designated accountability partner to see if any adult sites have been visited. In an effort to get the word out about their new ministry geared toward Christian men, NetAccountability purchased a highly visible billboard along one of the busiest highways in Dallas.

A few months earlier I had met the founder and designer of NetAccountability, Brandon Cotter, after a presentation he gave at the Every Man's Battle conference. Brandon and I connected and met for lunch a few weeks later, where I talked with him about my desire to share my testimony and shed more light on the growing problem of porn.

When national and local media began to pick up on the billboard, NetAccountability received an onslaught of requests for interviews from both radio and television stations. Often the media wanted to speak with someone in recovery for pornography addiction, so when a call came in and the media wanted a real-life story, NetAccountability called me.

The first television interview I did was with the ABC affiliate in Dallas. At the time I wasn't prepared to reveal my identity, so I did the interview anonymously. However, my closest friends recognized me, and later I found out that others knew that it was me as well, so word had spread about my porn problem.

After that interview I spent some time talking to Christina about what I felt God was calling me to do. She agreed with me but felt uncomfortable with going public so quickly. The wounds she had suffered were still quite tender, and the media attention would only pour salt in the wounds. But she assured me that she was with me and felt that indeed God was using my story to help others, so she agreed that I should do more media revealing my identity.

More calls came in, and before long I was asked to do an interview with the Associated Press. I called up my conference president and asked for the green light to do the interview. His response was that he would not forbid me from doing it—that it would be up to me. He told me that it would create controversy, and if I were willing to deal with it, then he would back me up. I didn't want to conceal my identity any longer. I had played that game for so long, and it didn't feel right.

The reporter even seemed surprised that I would use my real name and occupation as a pastor. That story was picked up all over the country and became the subject of radio talk shows and evening newscasts. One of my church members at the time commented to me that he heard my name mentioned on a radio talk show while driving home from work. Oddly enough, the subject matter didn't seem to bother him. He was more impressed that his pastor was on the radio!

Focus on the Family

In March 2004 I was invited to Colorado Springs to do an interview with Dr. James Dobson of Focus on the Family. Having read several of James Dobson's books over the years, I had come to admire his wisdom and counsel to families and adolescents. I had also heard Dr. Dobson speak passionately on his radio program about the issue of pornography and the devastating impact porn has on families. Now I was coming to personally meet him and share my own story of porn's damaging effects with listeners all over the world.

The guests on the panel that day included two therapists. Just prior to taping the show we spent about 10 minutes in Dr. Dobson's office visiting. He was very gracious and sincere in our interaction and seemed genuinely interested in who we were and what we were bringing to the show. We all felt very much at ease heading into the studio taking our positions behind the microphones. The taping went smoothly, and it turned out that we recorded enough of our discussion that it was used for two programs.

While James Dobson is a lightning rod on some political and social issues, in my brief time with him I found him to be a genuine Christian man who is passionate about his convictions. After

I returned from doing the interview, I wrote to Dr. Dobson to express my appreciation for being part of his radio show. Within a few days I received a personal letter from him expressing gratitude to me for sharing my story.

Newsweek, Fox News, *Montel*

The April 12, 2004, *Newsweek* article titled "Preachers and Porn" is probably where most people became aware of my story. Before that issue of *Newsweek* hit the newsstands, I e-mailed friends, family members, and colleagues to share what was going on. I also personally called those closest to me who would be impacted by the story. I had a great deal of anxiety over whether or not to do an interview with a major national newsmagazine that wouldn't particularly be interested in the "testimony" but more of the dirt.

After seeking counsel from colleagues and friends, I agreed to do it. Once again I sensed that this would be an opportunity to pull back the layers of secrecy on the issue. There was also something powerful about telling the story, realizing that it would literally reach millions of people. It provided strength and confidence for me and further dulled porn's power in my own life. With a close friend by my side (who happens to be an attorney) I spent a couple hours with *Newsweek's* Chicago bureau chief. A day after the *Newsweek* article ran, I was contacted by a producer from Greta Van Susteren's show that airs on Fox News; they were also interested in doing an interview. Again, I was somewhat fearful of doing the interview but felt that it would make a difference and bring attention to the issue, so I agreed. There were important stories going on in the news around that time, so the producers chose not to air the interview.

When you go public, some people begin to think that you are some kind of media hound chasing after every opportunity to be in the spotlight. That wasn't what I was after at all. So when *The Montel Williams Show* contacted me and offered to immediately fly my wife and me to New York to tape a program, I declined to be part of the show.

Dream Kids Inc.

Making my story public not only impacted my family and pastoral ministry but it also would have an impact on the organization I founded during seminary. Receiving inspiration from participating in Andrews University's student-led Benton Harbor Street Ministries project, I determined that I would create an organization that would send children from low-income families to Christian summer camps around the country. With my years of summer camp experience and the broad network of camps that I had been exposed to over the years, I felt that this would be a powerful ministry to unchurched kids. I talked to Christina about it and aside from the normal fears of launching a new ministry she was totally onboard and thrilled about the idea of helping children.

Christina played a major role in the organization especially after we returned from Michigan. Her job was to connect with the children and their families and prepare them for camp. Since we sought to support kids from any urban area in the country, this proved to be a very challenging and exhausting process for her.

My job was to raise funds and network with camps and potential donors. We received quite a bit of exposure in the local Dallas-Fort Worth media and even some national attention when our organization was mentioned in *Parade* magazine. During this time we received a grant from the Dallas Mavericks NBA team and a donation from the foundation created by the owner of the Dallas Cowboys, Jerry Jones. Working with Dream Kids was such an exciting time for us and we felt that God used our organization to impact the lives of so many kids. Once my story was made public I felt it would be important to pull back from Dream Kids both from a public relations perspective but also to concentrate on my family and the process of recovery.

———————

My head elder at the time my story went public told me that a friend said to him something along the lines of "Anyone who would talk publicly about a problem in this area has to be either crazy or very courageous!"

From my perspective, I would say it was a little of both. It really does go against logic to willingly put yourself in the position I did. In my case, I had not been caught publicly. No one had found anything on my computer, and I hadn't been caught in any compromising situations at my church office. My reputation was solid, and I was well-liked by members and administrative officials. It seemed that everything a young, up-and-coming pastor wanted to have going for him was happening for me. No one besides my wife and the pastor I confided in knew about my problem, and I could have kept it that way.

There are several reasons I chose to speak out publicly. First, my life was changed. More than anything else, people had to hear a story—a testimony, if you will—of Jesus' power to change even a pastor's life. In the same way that Jesus had set people free during His ministry on earth, He had set me free, and it seemed ridiculous to keep it to myself. Second, I had always struggled with the thought that I must be the only guy that has this problem. And most certainly I must be the only pastor who hides this secret. But through the process of becoming educated on this issue, I became aware that porn is a widespread problem, even among Christians. I also learned that keeping quiet about it only seems to fuel the fire. Being familiar with the culture of my particular denomination, I knew that we haven't always been the best at dealing with the ugly side of life in the way that we should. The tendency is to masquerade as though no one has any problems or issues—and if they do, they'd better take care of them before they come to church.

So this was a total counterculture move on my part. I sensed God leading me to create a bit of discomfort (kick the hornet's nest) by honestly and openly talking about my problem. I knew that the fact that I was a pastor would perhaps make my story more compelling. I wanted to send a clear message to the church that we needed to address this issue and not contribute to its growth by concealing it. I knew that the power of sexual sin is in its secrecy, and as long as we ignored it, there would continue to be casualties.

Some have misinterpreted my honesty on this issue as an attempt to bring down the church and cast a negative light upon our pastors and leaders. That hasn't been my intention at all. In fact, whenever I share my story somewhere, I talk about how my church has stood by me in all of this. How members and leaders have called me with words of encouragement, even grateful that I came forward the way I did. Granted, I have lost some friends over this whole thing, and some people have distanced themselves from me. Sometimes it is a bit awkward approaching a friend or colleague I haven't seen in a while, wondering if there's still a relationship. I do grieve the loss of connection with some, but I wouldn't change how I've handled things.

At one point I scribbled a quote in a notebook: "I would rather be admired than known." I'm not sure who said it, but that pretty much described me. Any prominence or popularity I had gained in ministry was based somewhat on a false premise. I don't discount anything God had used me to do in ministry prior to this, but I would say that people weren't seeing the entire picture. Going public allowed me to make the point that I was more interested in authenticity than popularity—which I think is an important place to arrive at. It no longer mattered so much what people thought about me. The conviction that God placed on my heart was to speak out, even at the cost of losing my job.

To close this chapter, let me share another clear indicator to me of God's leading. The CBS affiliate in Dallas ran a feature piece on my story during what media people call "sweeps" week. This is the time of year when television stations attempt to attract the largest numbers of viewers and gain the highest ratings. A reporter named Jack Fink got ahold of the *Newsweek* article and wanted to do a story on me. On the night the story ran, Jack Fink did a live report in front of my church, saying, "He's passionate about helping others overcome the same addiction." When the shot went back to the anchor in the studio, he made a comment that blew me away: "Turning something bad into something good." That's the message I hope you'll hear as well.

★ "The Leadership Survey," *Leadership Journal,* Winter 2001, p. 89.

FINDING OUR WAY BACK

"Trust in the Lord with all your heart and lean not on your own understanding; in all your ways acknowledge him and he will make your paths straight."—Proverbs 3:5, 6.

"Hold on to instruction, do not let it go; guard it well, for it is your life." —Proverbs 4:13.

The challenge with writing a story of personal turnaround and deliverance from addiction is the danger of leaving the impression that I've been cured and am now immune to the lure of pornography. One could also get the impression that after only a brief period of anguish, it was simply a matter of finally giving my sin problem over to God. Words such as "surrendered," "free," "victory," and "overcame" can be disheartening for many out there who have taken their problem or addiction to God countless times, only to continue to fall off the wagon.

I don't want to diminish in any way God's restorative work in my life. As anyone who's found freedom after a longtime struggle knows, deliverance is quite miraculous. But neither do I want to leave the impression that I'm totally immune to my vulnerability to pornography. Testimonies that come across triumphant and imply complete cure always make me a bit uneasy.

Yes, I enjoy the freedom that I know, and I'm not white-knuckling it, but I am painfully aware of my own weakness. It would be a greater tragedy if you were to read my story and walk away feeling as if somehow my prayers were answered while yours went ignored. If you're struggling, I pray that as you read, you don't get the impression that there is no way, given your many attempts, that you can ever break free. That, I believe, is a lie perpetrated by Satan himself and is designed to discourage and further entangle anyone God is moving toward recovery.

The truth is that we're all "broken" and will be until the King returns to restore us completely. Therefore, while I may experience (by God's power) God's restorative work, I'll still remain vulnerable as a fallen being. That doesn't mean I'm constantly on the edge of some terrible sinful act, but it does mean that Satan is relentless in his pursuit of our destruction, and to ignore that, or walk around as if we are untouchable, is to set oneself up for failure. That may be discouraging to those who believe they've achieved some level of immunity against sin of any sort. But for me, I'm constantly made aware of my total and complete dependence upon Christ for everything, especially sexual integrity. Apparently false pride and self-righteousness don't really get us anywhere:

"When pride comes, then comes disgrace, but with humility comes wisdom" (Proverbs 11:2).

"Pride goes before destruction, a haughty spirit before a fall" (Proverbs 16:18).

In my case, things did turn around rather quickly, and I'm incredibly grateful, but by no means am I cured. I still live with the vulnerability to act out with pornography. While I haven't returned to pornography since my decision to pursue purity, more than once I've come across Internet links that would have led down that forbidden path. I've sat staring at junk e-mail that I knew would lead to an adult site, wanting to click on it, only to think of the consequences of such an action and have them outweigh the short-term pleasure of indulging.

I've found myself playing those games and telling myself, "I'll just check it out," as if to impose some sort of cruel test of my sobriety. I've even occasionally caught a glimpse of a voluptuous swimsuit model or an underdressed celebrity from a sports or entertainment Web site. Even during an innocent Google search, in the back of my mind I've found myself hoping that some random, racy picture would pop up. I haven't ventured back down the path of pornography, but occasionally I've found myself looking for the trailhead! No, in a real sense I still struggle with pornography, but it isn't the stronghold that it once was.

Sexual integrity, of course, goes far beyond abstinence from pornography. So if you've been thinking all along that you don't have "that" problem, think again. Believe it or not, some men don't struggle with pornography (Internet, magazines, DVDs, etc.) at all. I've talked to guys who really don't understand the draw, and aside from the occasional dirty e-mail from a coworker, it rarely interferes with their lives. But some of these same guys have a hard time saying no to any opportunity to hop in the sack with a willing partner. These same guys can't help craning their necks to see a bouncing jogger on the side of the road. Or they can't keep their eyes off the low-cut blouse of the receptionist during an office visit.

Losing the Labels

I'm also concerned about the person who chooses to remain labeled by their sin after experiencing God's work through recovery. The opposite end of the spectrum is to so closely identify yourself with the sin that it provides a ready excuse when you fall back into a destructive cycle. It becomes easy to tell yourself, "Well, I'm an addict—that's what addicts do!" Some addicts struggle through years of attending group meetings or try many different recovery programs to achieve and maintain sobriety. They never really break free, in part because they can't cut loose from the constant shadow of their addiction branding. Some actually thrive off of the addiction community, becoming, in a sense, groupies, and foster an unhealthy dependence.

There is some debate among secular experts as well as Christian psychologists and counselors, as to whether or not someone should or should not refer to themselves as an addict. I'll leave the big debate to the experts, but clearly there are levels of involvement in pornography and other sexual sin. I see a real difference between the guy who masturbates occasionally when he receives his annual issue of the *Sports Illustrated* swimsuit edition and the guy who can't keep himself from spending hundreds or even thousands of dollars on pornography, strip clubs, and prostitutes. Then there's the woman who reads romantic stories and might fantasize for a few hours or even days about some guy she met, but she's far from being an addict.

From my experience I've seen that there is a small percentage of men who really aren't impacted at all by pornography. Then there are others who have a minimal weakness to porn and masturbation whereby it becomes something they occasionally do to relieve stress or simply entertain themselves. Then there are men and women who regularly look at porn, fantasize, and masturbate habitually, both to relieve stress and for sexual fulfillment, and also because they find sex with self extremely gratifying. They've essentially given in to the "flesh" and cannot live without that stimulation, even though it interferes with their career, family, or church. Clearly their lust has grown out of control. With the last group, pornography, fantasy, and masturbation may escalate and lead to an affair, debt, explicit chat rooms, exhibitionism, public exposure, or voyeurism. In other words, from my perspective they are more likely to be considered a "sex addict," and it may take years of accountability, therapy, and spiritual guidance.

In *Every Man's Battle* Stephen Arterburn suggests that most Christian men who struggle with pornography have a "fractional addiction." That means that it won't require years of therapy or group meetings, but in most cases freedom comes over a period of months. He further describes the levels of addiction by using a bell curve. "Another way of looking at the scope of the problem is to picture a bell curve," he says. "According to our experiences, we figure around 10 percent of men have no sexual-temptation problem with their eyes and their minds. At the other end of the curve, we figure there's another 10 percent of men who are sexual addicts and have a serious problem with lust. They've been so beaten and scarred by emotional events that they simply can't overcome that sin in their lives. They need more counseling and a transforming washing by the Word. The rest of us comprise the middle 80 percent, living in various shades of gray when it comes to sexual sin."[1]

Don't get me wrong. I'm not saying that there aren't addicts. There are, and we should use the terminology where appropriate. And I'm certainly not saying that the 12-step programs don't work. What I'm saying is that people who struggle don't have to be saddled with the addict label forever, and some don't need to be called an addict at all. It's certainly correct to use that label where clinically appropriate, but I think at some point, especially for someone well into recovery, they can start removing the label of addict.

Sure, I know that there is a fear that if a person in recovery doesn't refer to himself or herself as an addict, it is an open door to overconfidence, spiritual pride, and ultimately relapse. Yet I would say that the Holy Spirit makes the difference, and the same Spirit that keeps every Christian from becoming prideful about any area of their life can keep the recovering addict in check as well. When we come to Christ, we receive a new name—in fact, we are called His sons and daughters. No matter what we do, we are still considered His children. For some, it is time to lose the labels that tie them to their most glaring sin.

Fears

Since fear is a major culprit in the battle for sexual purity, it needs to be addressed early in the battle. The irony in my story is that fear kept me in bondage, and fear now keeps me free. What I mean is that the fear described in Genesis, after Adam and Eve sinned, is what kept me in bondage. That, I believe, is a fear that we inherited from our first parents. Genesis 3:9, 10 describes it this way: "But the Lord God called to the man, 'Where are you?' He answered, 'I heard you in the garden, and I was afraid because I was naked; so I hid.'"

This is an unhealthy, ungodly fear that leads us down a path toward hiding and isolation, just like it did with Adam and Eve. It is a shame-based, fig leaf fear that will never allow us to fully experience radical transformation through the Holy Spirit. Since the time that fear was introduced in the garden through sin, we've been dealing with its chief by-product—shame.

Yet Jesus was our example when He refused to allow the shame heaped on Him to control Him. Hebrews points to the shame of the cross as Jesus' defining moment. Hebrews 12:2 says that He "endured the cross, despising the shame" (NKJV). In other words, all that Jesus encountered—the beating, the name-calling, the public humiliation, the scorn—He would not accept. The Greek word for despised used in Hebrews 12:2 means to "take lightly" or literally to "look down on."

In verse three of chapter 12, the writer of Hebrews tells us, "Consider him who endured such opposition from sinful men, so that you will not grow weary and lose heart." What are the implications of this text for someone trapped by fear and shame because of pornography or other sexual sin? I think it has to mean that whether our shame is because of something we've done or something that's been done to us, we don't have to accept it. Looking to Christ, we can walk out of the darkness and into a place of openness and transparency. Obviously, this has to be done in a safe environment—you don't want to go throwing your story around to just anyone. Perhaps it begins with your spouse, a trusted friend, or a pastor. I believe that God has someone whom we can begin to open up to and finally ditch the fig leaves.

Another fear I have experienced is the respect that I have for God. It is what the Bible writer means when he says, "Fear God and give him glory, for the hour of his judgment has come" (Revelation 14:7). Another way to put it would be honor, reverence, and awe.

This fear comes only after we've tasted the depths of our own depravity and emerged from it at the hand of Christ. We come to a point of recognizing God's glory, and we stand in awe of Him. Even while the process may be painful, it may be what it takes for us to truly see Him. This fear is what every believer needs to experience, regardless of whether or not they've squandered their lives in some reckless form of debauchery. I like to think of it as being grounded in Christ, or levelheaded in Christ. This fear leads to obedience, rather than excuses and dodging.

We can be our own worst enemy. In my case I was afraid of the fallout of seeking help. The same might be true for you. The fear of letting someone know of your secret escapades to the local massage parlor or adult video rental store may be too much for you to bear—so you remain in hiding. But in your heart you know that you're not living the life you were meant for. Your story isn't meant to play out the way it has. Again we can look to the garden experience and see the promise that God would use to bridge the chasm created by Adam and Eve's sin: "And I will put enmity between you and the woman, and between your offspring and hers; he will crush your head, and you will strike his heel" (Genesis 3:15).

God's promise not only sealed the fate of the serpent (the devil), but it also created a way out of tragedy. That which was lost would be recovered, and ultimately the relationship that human beings enjoyed with God would be renewed. As God's children, we *have* been recovered, and we're the object of our Father's affection. Like a good parent, our heavenly Father wants only the best for us.

God on Our Side

That's what being a father is all about, isn't it? A father wants the best for his children, and he doesn't want them to be afraid. When each of my children were born, I did something for them and perhaps more so for my wife. On the day that each came home from the hospital I ordered a long, white stretch limousine for them to travel from the hospital to our house. Each one of my kids got to ride home in chauffeur-driven luxury. Granted, my newborns had no clue what was going on—it didn't matter to them if they were being driven in a Lincoln stretch limo or an AMC Gremlin! That didn't matter to me, because what I wanted everyone else to know was that someone thinks these people are very special. A chauffeur-driven limousine doesn't even begin to compare to what God wants for you and me. He's on our side, and He's for us! He doesn't discard us because we have failed. He still invites us to come and experience His best.

A limo is a bit extravagant, sure, but so is the fuss God makes over each one of us. *"In him we have redemption through his blood, the forgiveness of sins, in accordance with the riches of God's grace that he lavished on us with all wisdom and understanding"* (Ephesians 1:7, 8). God didn't, and still doesn't, cut any corners when it comes to His children. Those who subscribe to a fear-tactic mentality toward God are missing the boat. God doesn't use fear to inspire devotion; He uses love and incomprehensible grace.

You or someone you know may be feeling as though there is no way out, no way to recover from something so deeply ingrained. I've been there, and I can tell you that I never thought I would see the day that I would live without pornography and masturbation. I thought I would take my secret struggle to the grave. But I won't. The truth is that God sympathizes with the underdog. He knows when we're outmatched, undersized, and outmuscled, and He'll come to our aid if we let Him. Second Chronicles 16:9 tells us, "For the eyes of the Lord range throughout the earth to strengthen those whose hearts are fully committed to him."

We're no different from the people whose stories are told in the Bible. Men and women such as Gideon, Esther, David, and even the entire kingdom of Israel found themselves facing obstacles that were insurmountable without God. And it was in those instances that God revealed Himself as a God who takes pleasure in supporting His children. Granted, just as I was, you're likely the one who got yourself into such a mess. The pleasure of sexual sin renders us practically insane, but you haven't strayed so far that God won't zero in on your plea for forgiveness and help.

You're Not Alone

Without a doubt, the specific problem of pornography is growing among Christians. A 2006 poll conducted by two Christian organizations found that 50 percent of all Christian men and 20 percent of Christian women are addicted to pornography.[2] Sadly, with the emergence of the Internet in the nineties—and the convenience and anonymity offered by Internet pornography—many casual users of porn have found themselves propelled into a deeper, darker addiction.

Women and Pornography

The surprising trend is the growing consumption of pornography by women. Porn has generally been seen as a male-only problem, yet women young and old are becoming entangled. It is easy for me to focus on men, but I don't want to give the impression to the women reading this that they are somehow inoculated against the lure of sexual temptation. First, I think it is appropriate to acknowledge that Christian women have a libido too. So often we forget the fact that women were created with sexual desire just as we guys were. In general, however, the temptations are different for women. Since women enjoy an emotional connection and romance, sex for them often begins with talking. Women tend to be vulnerable when they sense that a man is more concerned about who they are internally than what they may have to offer physically.

Fantasy tends to be the main area women struggle with. In an article for *Today's Christian Woman* Ramona Richards remarks on the way women relate to pornography and where it can ultimately lead: "Women desiring to find companionship often prefer cybersex and online chat rooms to porn sites that offer only pictures and graphic stories, but they eventually start surfing both. All forms of pornography can stimulate the user, releasing chemicals in the brain that act on the body in much the same way as cocaine does. It's an exhilarating but unfortunately short-lived euphoria. The loneliness returns, leaving the woman wanting more contact and more stimulation, thus creating the cycle of addiction."[3]

Men, especially, have to be honest about this stuff. We know that our current culture isn't going to do us any favors. We have to live with suggestive beer ads, the bare middriff fashion trend, hip-hugging low-cut jeans, racy billboards, sexual-innuendo-filled sitcoms, and Victoria's Secret "fashion" shows. The reality is that things aren't going to get any better. So if you're waiting for the flood of sensuality to recede, you'll be waiting a long time. If you're waiting for some type of reprieve before you start your comeback, it's not going to happen.

No doubt about it—the journey back demands much from us. I'm convinced that the reason so many miss out on transformation is because they believe that it simply happens because we *want* it to—in other words, we assume that it's a totally passive experience that happens gradually over a period of time without our knowing it. The truth is that your—and my—comeback will be the result of consistent, intentional activity aimed at enhancing our relationship with God and those closest to us.

While growing up I was a big fan of the *Rocky* movies, and even today I still like the comeback story. Played by Sylvester Stallone, Rocky is an unlikely hero and champion. He isn't as quick as other boxers, and he doesn't really have the physical makeup to withstand a heavyweight bout. But what sets Rocky apart is his heart and his passion to be a champion. It means that Rocky has to train more and train harder than any other fighter. It means that he will likely get knocked down, so he'll have to know how to take a punch and get back up.

The same is true for you and me. Alone we're no match for pornographers or pornography. They're on the cutting edge of technology, always looking for new delivery systems for their product. So if you and I go into the ring casually, unconcerned, halfheartedly, we will fail. But like Rocky's beloved old coach, Mickey, we have a coach, a helper, who will guide us through the battle if we'll only let Him. Understand that it isn't so much about you trying harder as it is about you hearing and responding to what God wants you to do. In my experience, I tried harder and *harder*—and it got me nowhere. It isn't that we achieve freedom through performance enhancement. We may achieve abstinence, but abstinence isn't the only goal—transformation is. Authentic transformation comes as a result of the complete reorientation of our life and priorities.

It's Not Over

You might feel as though you've run out of chances with God, but I promise that He hasn't given up on you. That goes contrary to His character as Savior. He never writes people off. And you can't be written off either. If you are still aboveground and haven't been laid to rest yet, then there is still hope.

After I shared my story publicly, some people told me (or confessed to others) that they were totally embarrassed by my revelation. In many cases their problem wasn't as much the pornography as that I chose to be so public about it. I've even lost friends over my public confession, and there are others who won't return my phone calls or e-mails. I received one letter from a woman who expressed her exasperation by saying, "Didn't you realize that *Newsweek* goes all over the world!" I immediately wrote back and shared my sincere appreciation that she would take the time to write.

But after considering her embarrassment and what others said about being turned off by my story, the thought occurred to me, *Shouldn't the Bible embarrass them too?* A not-so-careful reading of the Bible (particularly the Old Testament) will reveal many "embarrassing" stories: David and Bathsheba; Abraham; Lot, and his own daughters; Samson and his failures. All these famous Bible heroes were once villains and failures—and they failed while they were in relationship with God. Why aren't we embarrassed by their stories? What has happened that they no longer make us blush? Why don't we just ignore those parts of the Bible and concentrate on the good stuff?

God included the stories of failure in the Bible because He wants us to see that there is hope for us, too. We can hardly embarrass God—He's seen it all. That isn't to make light of God's real disgust of our sin. God abhors sin in all its forms. But unlike us, He doesn't quickly condemn and write people off. The words in John confirm this: "For God did not send His Son into the world to condemn the world, but that the world through Him might be saved" (John 3:17, NRSV).

In my life as a pastor, people have told me many stories of their sin and failure. In one place a young woman (a church member) came to church drunk and reeking of alcohol. She actually brought alcohol with her, disguised in a plain plastic cup, and sipped it during the worship service. Later, she was completely embarrassed by what she'd done and confessed it all to me, apologizing profusely. I acknowledged that her behavior was disrespectful and completely irresponsible. But I also told her that I would rather she be an alcoholic *in* the church, and not hide it, than be one outside of the church and pretend to be OK.

Jesus didn't seem to be embarrassed by the sinners He spent time with, and God isn't embarrassed by your sin either. He wants to help you mount your comeback.

Grace

Our comeback is possible only because of grace. Grace is the gift of a second chance at a relationship. It's a startling gift. It comes with no strings attached. Grace comes out of nowhere—unexpected, unpredictable, and undeserved. It can't come any other way, or it wouldn't be grace. Grace is meant to be experienced. It's a precious, free gift, and once you pick yourself up after being accosted by grace, you can't help but leap and dance and even shout with joy and freedom.

The reason we need grace is because of the extent of our brokenness. The Bible speaks of our condition in Romans 3:23: "All have sinned and fallen short of the glory of God." In Psalm 51:5, David wrote, "Surely I was sinful at birth; sinful from the time my mother conceived me." According to Romans 5:12, "Therefore, just as sin entered the world through one man, and death through sin, and in this way death came to all men, because all sinned." Sin impacted the whole of humanity, haranguing us into a desperate situation that only the supreme sacrifice of God's only Son could remedy (John 3:16).

Since the integrity of our souls has been compromised from birth, we come to this life with certain vulnerabilities. Add to that any family tragedy, sexual trauma, neglect, abuse, or abandonment, and the small limp that we are born with can become a noticeable hindrance to our walk. Porn is deceptively soothing and therefore impersonates exactly what we desire—closeness and intimacy.

Satan uses porn to exploit our brokenness. Porn easily latches on to our already weakened souls, for our condition produces a legitimate longing for acceptance, love, kindness, and peace. Jesus comes to us as the only one who can and will fill that emptiness created by sin. He promises healing, restoration, and true intimacy. Listen to Malachi 4:2: "But for you who revere my name, the sun of righteousness will rise with healing in its wings. And you will go out and leap like calves released from the stall."

My goal for the second part of the book, with my story as a backdrop, is to offer some guidance, encouragement, and teaching to help you on the journey toward healing.

---

[1] Stephen Arterburn and Fred Stoeker, *Every Man's Battle*, p. 31.

[2] Second Glance Ministries and www.christianet.com, 2006.

[3] Ramona Richards, "Dirty Little Secret," *Today's Christian Woman* (online edition), September/October 2003, p. 58.

DRIVING FORCES

"He has made everything beautiful in its time. He has also set eternity in the hearts of men; yet they cannot fathom what God has done from beginning to end."—Ecclesiastes 3:11.

"'No weapon forged against you will prevail, and you will refute every tongue that accuses you. This is the heritage of the servants of the Lord, and this is their vindication from me,' declares the Lord."—Isaiah 54:17.

Now that you've read my story, you may be left with the same question my wife asked me when she first read the manuscript: "Why would a pastor, who had everything going for him, look at porn, risking his family and his career?" Her question challenged me to do what I'd been somewhat resistant to do. That is, to try to portray what's at the core or root of an obsession with pornography. Another friend critiquing my manuscript said that I should go deeper as well. They're right, of course.

Their concerns probe the question: What is the driving force behind someone such as popular hip hop gospel artist Kirk Franklin? He appeared on *The Oprah Winfrey Show* to tell how he had pillaged through a dumpster in the middle of the night, looking for the porn magazine he'd thrown away a few hours earlier. Or what about the highly successful and respected Utah doctor and medical professor caught with hundreds of pornographic images on his office computer? Why do men—pastors, teachers, enter-tainers, and politicians—risk family, career, and reputation to en-gage in lurid, secret, sexual fantasy?

Past Pain

I'm convinced that the thing that drives many toward the in-sanity of pornography is the desperate need to fill an emptiness left by pain from the past. That pain, in general, has to do with our relationships. Again, we return to that scene in the Garden of Eden, where our first parents enjoyed true intimacy and fellow-ship with God and with one another. The very last verse of Genesis 2 says, "And they were both naked, the man and his wife, and were not ashamed" (verse 25, NKJV). So where there was no sin, there was no shame, and thus humans lived in *dignity* and har-mony with God and one another.

In Genesis 3 we read how, through the serpent's deception and their choice, sin entered the world and Adam and Eve reacted in shame. "Then the eyes of both of them were opened, and they knew that they were naked; and they sewed fig leaves together and made themselves coverings" (verse 7). Verses 8 and 9 provide us with another glimpse into the shame they felt: "And they heard the sound of the Lord God walking in the garden in the cool of the day, and Adam and his wife hid themselves from the presence of the Lord God among the trees of the garden." Verse 10 says: "So [Adam] said, 'I heard Your voice in the garden, and I was afraid because I was naked; and I hid myself.'" By the end of chapter 3 (verse 24) humans are driven out of the garden from their place of *dignity* to a place of *depravity*. Since that time hu-manity has been on the run from God and from each other, choosing isolation and distance as fig leaves to cover up the wound from our fall. It's important to understand two aspects of sin. It's likely that you were taught, as I was, that sin is the "trans-gression of the law," and that's true. But sin happens in two forms: sins of commission and sins of omission. Sins of *commission* are things that we do—our actions that go contrary to God's commands. Sins of *omission* are the things that we fail to do that God would have us do. Unfortunately, they often work in conjunction with one another.

Take a pastor so dedicated to ministry that he fails (omission) to demonstrate affection and love to his children and spouse because he is too busy caring for his church members. Eventually his children grow to resent both the church and their father because he has failed to engage himself in their lives. Perhaps the pastor's daughter meets a young man, and they start a relationship. It turns out that the young man isn't good to the daughter—in fact, he's verbally abusive (commission), controlling, and interested only in taking advantage of the girl for sex.

After a while the young girl gives in (commission) to the young man's pressure for sex. She forms a soul-bond with this rebellious boy, which makes it harder for her to break up with him. But the abusive language continues and becomes physical. Eventually the young girl finds out that her boyfriend has been cheating on her, but now she's emotionally dependent upon him and feels that someday she can even change him, so she stays in the relationship. Ultimately the daughter lives with a distorted self-image, believing that she is worthless and undeserving of true love. She does things that she would have never thought she would do in order to feel loved. She feels dirty and defiled. Eventually she does break away from her relationship with this young man, only to fall into similar relationships throughout her life.

Tragically, what has happened is that the father's sins of omission (failure to provide guidance and nurture in a meaningful way), coupled with the young man's sins of commission, and mingled with the daughter's legitimate, innate desire for true intimacy created a volatile, unhealthy relationship. The shame we feel from those sins committed against us, as well as those we willingly carry out on our own, reveal a wound that we may spend a lifetime attempting to bandage or medicate using food, drugs, or sex.

As a father and the pastor, in this case, I should have been there all along to demonstrate true love, and affection as a living example of how a man should treat a woman. This type of interaction from a father with his daughter is invaluable for a young girl entering adolescence and adulthood. Not only that, but a father has to be there to run interference for his daughter when it comes to discerning the character of young men who show an interest. If father and daughter have bonded, then the daughter will be appalled by any attempts to take advantage of her—because she'll understand that her father has shown her what true care and love are like. So to experience anything else would clearly be seen for exactly what it is—a sham!

Dr. Harry Schaumburg offers some important thoughts on sin's impact on our relationships, which ultimately leads to a distortion of our sexuality. In his classic work *False Intimacy,* he writes, "The consequences of the Fall on human sexuality are of immense significance in understanding sexual behavior. On the broadest level, the Fall resulted in our maleness and femaleness being threatened. We became naked and ashamed of our sexuality. The Fall impacted all ensuing relationships, and thereby all sexual relationships."[1]

We know that Jesus promises to forgive our sins, and by His grace and mercy that's true. But the problem comes when we are victims of sin. While there is forgiveness and cleansing for those sins that we commit, what about the sins committed against us? What if we are victims of sinful acts? No doubt there is forgiveness in those instances as well, but very often the damage has already been done. Some of the more devastating acts of sin committed against others are sexual molestation, abuse, rape, and extreme neglect. The words are difficult even to write, but it's true that even within a church community these horrific things have occurred. Yes, we know that God can cleanse us from the defilement that we experience from any sins committed against us, but it takes time to become convinced that we are lovable, accepted, and desired by both God and others.

The following comments, e-mailed from a friend who has battled sex addiction for the better part of his life, further reflect the damage often done by others:

"My biggest issue in life has been my deep sense of emasculation, which came as a result of the sexual abuse I experienced, my mother's abuse and control, and my father's abandonment. I believed that I was somehow inherently inferior to other men and that all men had something that I was missing. I confronted those lies and was affirmed by God that I do possess the very essence of masculinity—divine masculinity—because I possess the ability to show compassion, forgiveness, and mercy instead of hatred and resentment. I traded in my old label of 'emasculated and weak' for 'Warrior and Priest of my home.' I was also able to forgive my father and release him from his debt to me (from not fathering me). I choose to believe God's promise that He will re-father me in all the ways my own father did not."

My friend describes a common experience of men as they relate to their fathers. Gordon Dalbey in his book *Father and Son* offers some insights on the negative impact of the separation of a father and son:

"That wound is caused by an epidemic alienation from the father, who is every man's masculine root in this world. This breach in the masculine soul is the gateway for destruction both in and through men today. The powers of the world, however, do not want to recognize it, because they have no power to heal it. The father-wound can only be healed by the One sent by the Father God to do just that, namely Jesus, whom the world 'did not recognize' (John 1:10).[2]

"In a word, the boy today has not bonded with Daddy. Lacking that essential external connection to the larger world of men cripples his identification with the masculine in himself; his masculine courage and strength, associated negatively with the absent or destructive father, focus negatively. Muscles designed to protect, serve, and uplift are wasted in fistfights, anesthetized by alcohol and drugs, or paralyzed by fear. Manly presence and its call to truth and accountability—from meeting the girlfriend's father to facing a congressional ethics committee—is often simply gone: the girlfriend's father may be lost to a TV ball game or divorced and living elsewhere; the congressmen themselves may lack ethics."[3]

Our experience, then, is that we were born in *dignity* into the likeness and image of God, but through sin we fell into *depravity*, which then led to *defilement* both from those things we have done and things that have been done to us.[4]

Temporary Escape

Another driving force behind much of the culture's vulnerability toward porn can be traced to the simple fact that we live in a digital age in which men and women are constantly bombarded with sexual images. Many even from healthy backgrounds with healthy relationships still fall prey to the lure of porn simply because of the almost continual bombardment of sensual material. Pornography, like other sin, offers pleasure and a temporary escape from the sometimes dull and mundane routine of life. In a similar way that a drug has the power to temporarily transfer you from this world to another, pornography is the ultimate getaway experience for the unsuspecting consumer. A licensed therapist that I heard speak on the topic of pornography addiction said that he sees a high percentage of clients who have *not* experienced any deep emotional trauma, yet are dealing with this issue. It is the tragic result of the immense reach of porn into the lives of so many people.

We all long for someone in our corner. We long to know that someone genuinely cares for us no matter what. We know that our heavenly Father cares for us, and we are taught that He will never leave us nor forsake us. But we also need earthly affirmation from those around us. I heard a story about a little girl who was terrified by a thunderstorm and called out to her daddy as she lay cowering under the bedcovers in her room. Her father quickly came to her bedside and encouraged her that she could pray and that Jesus would be by her side protecting her from the storm. He went to his room, but just a few minutes later the little girl called out again, "Daddy, Daddy, I'm still afraid!" Her father returned to her room once again, reassuring her that Jesus was with her and would take away her fear of the storm when she prayed. Finally the child plainly told her dad, "Daddy, I know Jesus will be with me, but I need someone with skin!" It is so true that we all need people with "skin" as we make our way through this life.

This is certainly where churches should invest more time, training, and money to help create communities that care for and nurture those who come into our midst. Our churches should reflect Paul's attitude in 1 Thessalonians 2:8, where he refers to his personal affection for those he shared the gospel with: "We were well pleased to impart to you not only the gospel of God, but also our own lives, because you had become dear to us" (NKJV). Paul and his companions recognized the importance of connecting to those they ministered to in such a personal way that they were even vulnerable enough to share other parts of their lives. And that's where transformation takes place. As the truth of the gospel is revealed through the caring lives of those who impart it, lost and hurting people respond.

People come with all sorts of wounds that lie at the root of their sin problems. And, granted, the local church is rarely equipped to handle much of what could surface if we probe deeper, but that shouldn't hinder us from creating an environment that allows for transparency and authenticity. The church doesn't have to be, and likely cannot be, the place where people receive professional therapy to deal with wounds from their past—or, for example, if they've been lured into pornography by the mere fact that it's seemingly omnipresent. But the church may be the place that allows for those things to be revealed, leading a person to seek out both spiritual and professional support.

As I mentioned in the previous chapter, we make our way into this world with a deep longing to be loved and cared for. If we don't experience that, then we do our best to find it in some way, usually through a false form of intimacy. Again, Dr. Harry Schaumburg describes fallen humanity's desperation: "The Fall did not diminish our capacity for intimacy; it created a distortion and an agonizing disruption of intimacy. Each of us longs to break through the limitations of our existence into a blissful unending intimacy with others. Such a dream cannot, however, be fulfilled. So we desensitize our hunger and thirst for the pre-fallen state by preoccupying ourselves with career, family, food, sex, leisure, and other distractions. But no diversion can richly satisfy our souls. Inner emptiness, the result of original sin, lies just blow the surface of the illusion we create in order to cope with life."[5]

As I've come to grapple with this issue in my own life, I can look back on it and say that my wound stems from a sense of abandonment by my father. When one of the presenters at the Every Man's Battle workshop talked about this, he immediately struck a cord deep within me. In an instant I did a full evaluation of my life, honestly coming to terms with what had brought me to this place. I realized then and there that I had been unwilling to admit that indeed the absence of my father did hurt deeply. I came to realize that I was driven by that which I did not want to become. Yet in the quiet times when no one was looking, I longed for connection, fellowship, and attachment to someone bigger than I who cared for me. My pornography habit, then, was simply evidence of something deeper going on in my soul. But rather than honestly seeking connection, I took a shortcut with pornography because it provided an easier, less vulnerable way to find relief.

My parents were young when they had me, which wasn't altogether unusual in the time in which they grew up. Young people tended to enter adulthood a little more quickly back in those days. Anticipating the need for a more stable income, my father enlisted in the Navy. I'm certain that he chose that route in order to provide for his young family, but also to get an education and assure all of us a ticket out of our Arkansas community.

My mother worked various jobs while attending college to earn a nursing degree. I vaguely remember attending my mother's graduation and nurse pinning ceremony when I was a kid. My mother was raised in a rural area. When she wasn't picking cotton, she dreamed of being a teacher. She would carefully take her play dolls and set them up in chairs, pretending that they were the students in her class. To this day I am grateful to both my parents for setting an example by placing an emphasis on the importance of getting an education.

I greatly attribute my own personal drive for success and achievement to my parents. They were tenacious, almost to a fault, in their desire to be successful. Raised in a racially volatile South, they came of age at a time when it would have been easy for both of them to allow hatred and bitterness to become permanent roadblocks to their success—but they didn't. With an inborn ambition, they chose to go on the attack and achieve rather than wait for something to happen. My father (now retired) spent 30 years in the Navy, eventually climbing to the rank of commander. Considering where my dad came from and the color of his skin, that's an amazing accomplishment. He also went on to earn an M.B.A. and a Ph.D. My mother, who picked cotton as a teenager, is a registered nurse and entrepreneur, having started and run both a tailor shop and a restaurant. She has made her way through life with a courage and determination that's quite remarkable.

My parents' marriage came to an end after 12 years—around the time I was entering my teens. Until this point things were pretty normal and happy. I was involved in sports, we had regular family outings, and I spent time after school at the naval reserve base while my dad worked. Aside from the occasional arguments, things in our home were relatively stable. To this day I have never had a long discussion with either of my parents about why their marriage ended. I know the divorce rate among military families tends to be higher than that of the civilian population, so I'm guessing that my father's career aspirations played a major role in the breakup. After my parents divorced, I'm certain it must have been a difficult time, especially for my mother, who suddenly found herself a single mom with a teenage son to raise and keep out of trouble.

Concerned for my well-being, my mother enrolled me in a small private school not far from where we lived. I have no doubt that God led my mother to check out this little school run by the

Seventh-day Adventist Church. I entered Little Rock Adventist Academy in the fifth grade, never having heard of a Seventh-day Adventist or their stance on eating pork and their other distinctive standards. I remember walking into the school on the first day, sipping a cup of orange juice and eating a Sausage McMuffin with Egg from McDonald's. No one said anything about my dietary choices that day, but eventually I became very much aware of the Adventist Church's stance on pork, along with other cultural and doctrinal nuances.

My mother did the best that she could to make my life as normal and as happy as possible. She always wanted me to have the best things and go to the best schools. I know that she never wanted me to miss out on anything. And she never spoke maliciously about my father to me or tried to turn me against him. In fact, she wanted me to visit him, or him to visit me, as often as possible. Of course, it was difficult for this to happen since my dad was building a military career.

I'm positive that my dad never had any intentions of hurting me. He just didn't know how to handle what was going on. We rarely set out to intentionally hurt the ones we love, but if we aren't guided, that's just what will happen. Most devastating for me was that my dad never attempted to include me in what was happening with him and my mother—and he did not say goodbye when he left. As a kid, it was hard to deal with. My dad seemed so uninterested in my life. All I knew was that my father had abandoned me at a time when I so much wanted him there. Eventually I began to resent him and lose respect for him because I felt that he wasn't doing the responsible thing. I determined that *I* would never let anyone down. I would always be responsible and do the right thing. Going through that divorce created within me a desire to grow up and learn to make my way in this world without depending on anyone else.

Today my relationship with my father is amicable but not ideal. Since his retirement a few years ago he has pursued more opportunities to spend time with his grandkids, which has led to more interaction. We often connect over golf and whenever we are together we generally get a round or two in. Those feelings of resentment and even bitterness toward my father have subsided over time for me. I'm sure partly because I'm older now and raising my own children with a deeper appreciation for the fact that it isn't always easy to balance family and career.

The local Adventist church and school filled the void left by my absent father, and it was during this time that I turned to my heavenly Father. Perhaps it was through a sermon I heard at the Adventist church or something I read, but whatever the case, I remember making a conscious decision to have God become not only my heavenly Father but take the place of my earthly father as well. As a teenager, I found comfort in this, and it gave me great confidence knowing that God, my heavenly Father, would never leave me.

My decision was affirmed when I memorized my first scripture assignment in Bible class. It was 1 John 3:1-3 and began "Behold what manner of love the Father has bestowed on us that we should be called children of God . . ." (NKJV). This was truly an awesome discovery for me, and I knew for sure that God was with me and taking care of me. But there was also something in me that needed to mask the pain of the disappointment and loss I felt as a result of my parents' divorce and my father's absence. So not only did I adopt God as my earthly father, but I determined that the best way to avoid rejection would be to gain the approval of all.

So I became the life of every party. My personality lends itself to this anyway. It didn't hurt that being one of only a few Black students at the school, I naturally stood out. I'd also spent time playing tennis, basketball, and baseball, which gave me an immediate in with this new crowd. I was amazed at how sheltered most of the White students were from interaction with Blacks and other minorities. In some cases I was the first person of color many of them had ever been around!

Growing up in Arkansas, I had encountered racism and observed it at times in restaurants and other public places. But my parents never once allowed me the freedom to react in a negative or destructive way. They always conveyed to me that all people had equal worth and to say otherwise simply revealed one's ignorance. Rather than resorting to bitterness and violence, they emphasized the importance of always presenting oneself as educated. So I was never allowed to speak improper English. The controversy today over whether kids should be allowed to speak street language or what has become known as Ebonics played itself out in my family while I was very young. My parents were quite adamant about me speaking properly, clearly enunciating my words.

So for me as a Black kid entering a predominantly White school, speaking the way I did and being athletically inclined gave me ready acceptance. At times the fact that I moved so easily among the White students was a barrier to acceptance with other Blacks. My parents had always made a point of telling me to treat everyone the same, regardless of their race. And for me, I wanted the admiration and praise of everyone, regardless of the color of their skin. The church and school, in a sense, became a surrogate parent for me.

Yet it was during this time of adolescence that I was also trying to deal with my own sexuality without adult guidance. I never got "the talk" and had to wade through this powerful force all on my own. My education about sex was multifaceted. I heard a little from my cousins, and somewhere I discovered a book titled *The Joy of Sex*. I attempted to decipher what the joy was all about, but I was a bit distracted by the nude pictures. For the most part sexuality for me was just that—all about me. In youth Sabbath school we never approached the subject, yet a lot of us teens were noticing one another, and our talk often turned sexual.

I fear that my experience continues to be the norm for many churched young people. They've likely received the message from adults that sex outside of the context of marriage is bad and that they should abstain until then. But their bodies and their culture are sending them a different message. Teaching abstinence is important, but a healthy, godly perspective on sexuality is better—

especially since someday we don't *want* them to abstain.

Here's where we've often missed a grand opportunity as a church. At the critical moments of adolescence as our children are discovering sexuality, we give them the message that it's wrong—when, to them, everything about it seems right. Perhaps a better strategy would be to openly discuss the beauty and holiness of God's gift of sexuality. Rather than allowing the world to hijack sex and turn it into only a self-gratifying hedonistic activity, the church should reclaim it by revealing it as God's way for providing men and women with the ultimate expression of selflessness as they become united with a mate in marriage. We should tell them that it is good, healthy, and normal to have sexual desire because God created us with it. Thus we add substance to our call to preserve the experience of intercourse until marriage.

Things are even more complex today since young people are doing everything but having traditional vaginal intercourse. Oral and anal sex are now seen as a safe form of birth control. Teens, young adults, even 30-somethings are sexually active, but still claim their virginity because there hasn't been actual genital penetration. Pornography use among this demographic often fuels the fires of lust and desire.

At this point you might be saying, "OK, nice story, but what does it have to do with pornography?" I believe it has much to do with it. That isn't to say that our past has predestined us to a life of entanglement with pornography, but it is to affirm that whether positively or negatively, your past and mine have definitely shaped who we are today. We certainly don't want to dwell in the past, but it is wise to consider where we came from and what we've been through and to honestly consider the impact it has had on our life and personality.

Also, at some point perhaps we all should evaluate why we do the things we do. What has been the motivation for our accomplishments, and what drives us toward the goals that we've set for ourselves? My experience of self-discovery has provided me with a new perspective on my call to ministry and to serving the church. I am confident that God lead me to the place where I am today. Now I see that maybe He had a plan for me all along, and He didn't need for me to make myself more lovable in order to ensure His faithfulness. What about you? Are you afraid of failing, afraid of letting those around you down? Have you honestly considered what might be driving you toward unhealthy relationships, destructive habits, and poor choices? If the answer hasn't emerged yet, then maybe I've stirred something in you that will move you toward finding the answer.

---

[1] Harry Schaumburg, *False Intimacy*, p. 61.

[2] Gordon Dalby, *Father and Son*, p. 5.

[3] *Ibid.*

[4] Some of the thoughts here were inspired by a sermon by Pastor Mark Driscoll entitled "The Cross of Christ."

[5] Schaumburg, p. 30.

Chapter 10

THE POWER OF PORN

"Be self-controlled and alert. Your enemy the devil prowls around like a roaring lion looking for someone to devour."—1 Peter 5:8.

"O Lord my God, I take refuge in you; save and deliver me from all who pursue me, or they will tear me like a lion and rip me to pieces with no one to rescue me."—Psalm 7:1, 2.

On March 7, 1965, the Edmund Pettus Bridge in Selma, Alabama, was the scene of a gruesome attack that became known as Bloody Sunday. Nearly 600 mostly Black demonstrators marched in an effort to gain voting rights for all Blacks in that region. In an effort to show solidarity and raise awareness to their plight, leaders initiated a peaceful march that would take them from Selma to Montgomery, the state capital, crossing over the Edmund Pettus Bridge. But the demonstrators never made it any farther than the bridge. They encountered an armed force of state and local police officers outfitted with riot gear, some even mounted on horseback. The confrontation eventually erupted into a one-sided brawl, with the police using tear gas, bullwhips, and police dogs to turn the peaceful marchers back.

Today that bridge stands as a symbol of the struggle for freedom that many Blacks of that era endured. They desired to "get over" and find freedom, liberty, and justice on the other side. But what they encountered was extreme resistance and hostility that disrupted their courageous journey toward freedom.

In much the same way, our adversary, Satan, stations himself between us and our freedom. Satan stands as the opposing force determined to keep us in bondage. In John 10:10 Jesus describes him as the thief whose main objective is to steal, kill, and destroy. In contrast, Jesus says that He came that we might have life to the full. The enemy understands that freedom is powerful and is already a reality for the follower of Jesus. But as long as Satan peddles the lies and falsehoods about who we are, many men and women will continue to live a lie and remain slaves.

Satan's efforts to entrap and ensnare men sexually through pornography are an ever-present danger. Pamela Paul, a secular author, describes in her book *Pornified* just how immersed we are: "We're only beginning to recognize the implications of the growth in pornography and the pornified society's impact on individuals who live in it. We're only starting to grasp the extent to which the technology revolution of the past two decades has transformed the way in which porn is produced and consumed. Those who argue that pornography has been with us since cavemen first drew fornicating women on earthen walls ignore the vast discrepancies between a world in which pornography was glimpsed on the sly, where naked girls were glanced at on the faces of nudie poker cards, and today's culture, in which pornography is omnipresent, accepted, and glorified, and on an incessant advance."[1]

That pornography is "accepted," "glorified," and on the "advance" is substantiated by the fact that what used to be seen as abnormal and unacceptable has now become normal and embraced. The porn industry was once viewed as seedy and undesirable—yet today thousands of fans gather in Las Vegas for the AVN Adult Entertainment Expo (the largest porn show in the United States) for an up close encounter with their favorite porn stars. Mega porn stars such as Jenna Jameson, who wrote a book entitled *How to Make Love Like a Porn Star,* have easily bridged the gap between the taboo and the tame. Porn stars are making the transition to mainstream movies, and some who have amassed enormous amounts of wealth during their adult industry careers have branched off into other business ventures that have attracted the attention of mainstream media.

The new acceptance of porn can partly be attributed to the culture's overall obsession with sex, but a more telling indicator may be the fact that the spokespersons for the world have managed to tap into our depravity, taunting us to accept a message that the pleasure of sexual gratification is the pinnacle of what we can hope for in this life.

The "Paris Effect"

Take Paris Hilton, who was virtually unheard-of until a private home movie of her having sex with her boyfriend fell into the hands of someone who saw an opportunity to make money. The tape launched her into the spotlight, and overnight we were introduced to a young woman who has become the pop icon for everything sensual, sexual, and, as she describes it, hot. Pamela Paul makes a similar observation about Paris's rise to the top: "It's hard to imagine how, just 10 years ago, Paris Hilton, the (possibly unwitting) star of her own Internet porn clip, would have survived being thrust into cyberspace and forwarded with exponential speed. But Paris's foray into pornography pushed her further up the pecking order from B-list It Girl celebrity into one of the year's most promising stars."[2]

From her highly suggestive Carl's Jr. commercials to the more subtle, teasing romps with emaciated gal pal Nicole Richie on their hit reality TV show *The Simple Life*, Paris Hilton has emerged as a modern-day sex goddess worshipped by a culture awash in sexually explicit material.

The Bottom Line

In a word, pornography is all about the *money*. Pornographers and those who work in the industry are selling fantasy. They are smarter than we think and more calculated. They recognize that we live in a hypersexual culture in which appetites for sex are at an all-time high, and people are willing to pay a price. They also realize that people in our culture work harder and longer than ever, creating enormous amounts of stress that in turn generate a desire for an easy and frequent escape.

Consider that in 2006 the porn industry generated $100 billion worldwide and more than $13 billion in the United States. Those estimates surpass the revenues of the top technology companies, such as Microsoft, Google, Amazon, eBay, Yahoo, Apple, Netflix, and Earthlink.[3]

Distorted View

A remark made on the highly popular television show *Friends* reveals the impact porn can have on how men view life. In an episode titled "The One With the Free Porn," Chandler and Joey discover that they've tuned into a porn channel. And it's free! They leave the TV on, afraid that switching it off will mean no more pornography. By the end of the episode, Chandler is seeing the world through porn-tinted spectacles. "I was just at the bank," he complains, "and the teller didn't ask me to go do it with her in the vault." Joey, bewildered, reports a similar reaction from the pizza delivery girl. "You know what?" decides Chandler. "We have to turn off the porn."[4]

Imagine if we were to take a trip to the Louvre in Paris or the Getty Museum near Los Angeles. When we arrive and prepare to walk into the museum, I hand you a straw and tell you that you have to view all the incredible works of art through that straw. As you squint to view the beauty around you, you're unable to appreciate any of it because your view is too narrow and distorted. A similar thing happens to those who view pornography. Life begins to lose its color, vibrancy, brilliance. Everything one sees outside of porn is dull and boring. Nothing elicits the excitement of porn. Not even real sex! That's why some guys, deeply impacted by porn, can tell their wives that they aren't interested in them—

because they'd rather look at porn. Thankfully, God is able to heal our vision problems and restore our sight.

One-track Mind

Researchers are now beginning to look at porn's impact on the brain. Free-speech advocates have long scoffed at claims that pornography does significant damage to the consumer, claiming that religious leaders and other moralists are simply interested in suppressing the rights of mature adults who aren't confined by religious or moral views. Moreover, they assert that the scientific research for the claims that porn is harmful is severely lacking. But as you'll read below, research is now emerging that indicates that indeed real—physical—damage is done, especially to children and teens exposed to sexually explicit material.

Dr. Judith Reisman in her 2004 testimony entitled "The Science Behind Pornography Addiction," given before the U.S. Senate Committee on Commerce, Science, and Transportation, commented, "Thanks to the latest advances in neuroscience, we now know that pornographic visual images imprint and alter the brain, triggering an instant, involuntary, but lasting, biochemical memory trail, arguably, subverting the First Amendment by overriding the cognitive speech process. This is true of so-called 'soft-core' and 'hard-core' pornography. And once new neurochemical pathways are established, they are difficult or impossible to delete." Later in her testimony, Dr. Reisman commented on the vulnerability of children and youth. "This scientifically documented neurochemical imprinting affects children and teens especially deeply; their still-developing brains process emotions differently, with significantly less rationality and cognition than the adult brain."[5]

Dr. Gary Lynch, professor of psychiatry at the University of California at Irvine, commenting on how the brain processes information received from the outside world, says, "What we are saying here is that an event which lasts half a second . . . within five to 10 minutes has produced a structural change that is in some ways as profound as the structural changes one sees in [brain] damage."[6]

In Mark Kastleman's groundbreaking book, *The Drug of the New Millennium: The Brain Science Behind Internet Pornography Use: Three Power Principles Guaranteed to Protect Your Family*, he says:

"When an individual ingests or injects a 'drug,' that chemical travels to the receptors in the brain and other parts of the body, seeking to 'mimic' the body's own natural neurotransmitters. In effect, the drug tries to 'fake' the body into releasing its own natural or *endogenous* (produced from within) chemicals. For example, Prozac triggers the body to release its own natural serotonin. Likewise, . . . pornography 'mimics' sexual intimacy and 'fakes' the body into releasing a tidal wave of endogenous chemicals, (dopamine, norepinephrine, testosterone, oxytocin, etc.) which is exactly what pharmaceutical and illicit street drugs do. Should pornography not then be referred to as a 'drug'?"[7]

Finally in Laurie Hall's personal account of her husband's 20-year bout with pornography addiction, *An Affair of the Mind*, she comments on her suspicions about the damage she suspected porn had done to her husband's mind: "It wasn't until Jack and I were separated and we met with Dr. Ron Miller that my observations were verified. After examining Jack, Dr. Miller looked at him and said, 'You've destroyed your mind by fantasizing. You've dug a deep channel going in one direction. The rest of your mind is atrophied!'"[8] Any notion that pornography is just a harmless outlet for men and women to satisfy their natural sexual urges is clearly misguided.

Cyber Versus Physical

I've often been asked whether sexual sin through pornography was the same as an actual physical adulterous affair. I've usually answered in such a way that insinuates that unfaithfulness with pornography isn't quite as detrimental as the other, but I've changed my mind on that. Pornography, I would say, is as devastating to the marital relationship as a physical affair—or in some cases more devastating.

Now obviously sin is sin, and to measure instances of sexual sin in degrees is to an extent unnecessary. *But I do believe that there are degrees of impact of sin.* Some sins do greater damage than others experientially. My failure with pornography as a pastor does far greater damage than my failure in other areas of life. Further, when a husband strays with Internet porn, his mistress never leaves home! Computers will always be part of our lives—therefore, his spouse has an ongoing reminder of her husband's unfaithfulness. The wife may find that a lingering bitterness develops every time her husband spends vast amounts of time on the computer, even when it's for legitimate purposes. In a physical affair the same can happen, especially if the affair occurred between two people who attend the same church. But usually the wronged spouse doesn't have to see or be around the other party.

Additionally, the porn problem can be more difficult for the wayward husband to remove than an actual girlfriend. Once someone's mind has been immersed in the fantasy, it's difficult to return to earth—which then means a longer process of reconciliation. A physical affair is often overcome by separation and an out-of-sight, out-of-mind approach.

While the devastation from an online addiction and a physical affair may be equally damaging, that doesn't mean that looking at porn or having a cyber-affair is biblical grounds for divorce. In Matthew 5:28 Jesus provided a clear distinction between adultery of the heart (internal) and a physical affair (literal) when He said: "If anyone looks at a woman lustfully he has already committed adultery with her in his heart." Clearly both are sinful activities, but the consequences are different, and how we deal with the sin should be different. It would be the same as suggesting that 1 John 3:15 is implying that the person who hates his brother is just as guilty of murder as the person who actually physically committed that act of violence. Do we impose a prison sentence upon a person for having internal hatred toward someone? We have to conclude, then, that pornography, while a serious and damaging sin, does not constitute physical adultery and therefore does not provide biblical grounds for divorce. I would add, however, that over time a man or woman's refusal to deal with the sin problem might require a separation for the sake of children and the purpose of working toward reconciliation. Ultimately, if there is no change, then the relationship could end in divorce.

The Enemy at Work

The end of World War II came when Allied Forces stormed the beaches of Normandy with their D-day invasion. For the most part, the enemy was defeated on that day. But fighting continued for another year, and it was during that year that some of the bloodiest battles were fought and both sides suffered large numbers of casualties. In the mind of the enemy forces, they had nothing to lose. They were going down anyway, and they determined to take as many Allies down with them as they could. In much the same way, Satan is aware of the fact that he's beaten. He's beaten, but the war hasn't quite concluded yet. In a sense we live between D-day and the end of the war, and one of Satan's main weapons of choice in these critical moments before his sentence is carried out is to attack the gift of human sexuality.

The truth is that Satan isn't just "the" enemy; he's your personal enemy. In other words, he isn't out to get just the church—he's out to get *you* and multitudes of people like you. That may be why his attacks are on human sexuality and his weapon of choice is pornography. It can destroy hundreds and infect millions. It's more like an ongoing epidemic than a onetime major disaster. Just think about the fact that generations of fathers have passed down a legacy of porn use to their sons and, in some cases, even their daughters.

This is true even for those who come from churched backgrounds. I often counsel with Christian couples in preparation for their upcoming wedding. During the course of our sessions we talk about the sexual relationship. One of the questions I ask is "Where did your first information about sex come from?" After an awkward silence, one or both of them will often reveal that they discovered pornography in their home stashed underneath their parents' bed or in some other hiding place. In many cases, when this issue does surface, it was this unhealthy introduction to sexuality that created confusion and disillusionment about God's design for sex in marriage. However, when one or both say that they first learned about sex from porn, it provides an opportunity to talk about porn's detrimental impact on relationships—and ultimately God's disapproval of anything defiling or degrading in marriage.

It's like the man who shared his story with me a few years ago. He and his now ex-wife were both into pornography, and for a while it seemed as though he had it made. A wife who was into porn! He even told me how they would sit in church writing notes back and forth to each other about what issue of *Playboy* they were going to try to get later that evening. But slowly his marriage unraveled, and his dreamworld came tumbling down. The sexual adventure he and his wife were on could be sustained for only so long, and eventually it fizzled out. They found themselves making an appointment to see their pastor, but oddly enough they made a pact not to bring up the fact that they used porn in the bedroom! There's a real example of the deceptive nature of pornography.

If pornography is a weapon of mass destruction in our enemy's arsenal, then to begin to attack it or reveal it would be critical to saving many lives. And the enemy is not pleased to see this powerful weapon unmasked for what it truly is. He'll do whatever he can to conceal the true nature of pornography.

Youth

Statistics indicate that 80 percent of 15- to 17-year-olds have had multiple exposures to hard-core pornography. In the past, studies have indicated that 12- to 17-year-olds were the largest consumers of pornography, only recently having been surpassed by the 35-to-49 age group.[9] While there is no hard data to support the claim, many believe that the average age for a child to be exposed has now dropped to 5, contrasted to estimates prior to the emergence of Internet pornography, which were around age 11.

It would seem then that we need to turn our attention toward supporting young people in the battle for sexual purity. Popular Christian apologist, author, and youth speaker Josh McDowell says, "Rules without relationship lead to rebellion," and I think he's right on. Perhaps it isn't enough for the church to simply say, "Don't do it." Rather, we must begin to provide a reasoned response to the question so often raised by youth: "Why not?"

In order to answer that question with maximum impact, we must be in a trusting relationship with a teen. As a church, the most important strategy that we can employ will be to develop significant relationships with young people. In other words, our ministry and our message have credibility when they come through relationships. Young people are more likely to believe what you're saying if they deem you to be a credible source and know that you care. Regardless of your position in their life or the authority you may have, your impact will come as you form trusting relationships with young people.

That doesn't mean that we become a teenager again or compromise truth in an effort to relate. It *does* mean that we don't treat young people as some sort of subspecies that hasn't evolved to the same level as we have. It means that we'll have to connect with them in different settings outside of church, where they can see us with our hair down, so to speak. They need to see us as real people who not only talk a big game but demonstrate it daily in our lives.

I can remember the church attempting to warn us about the dangers of rock music and movies when I was a teen. At the end of a Week of Prayer or a spiritual retreat, the speaker often talked about being delivered from worldly music. In response, the kids who owned rock music would take their audiocassettes and smash them up, vowing to clean up their act for good. I'll never forget presentations that demonstrated how some of the lyrics of rock songs, when played backward, spoke satanic or sexual messages that targeted our subconscious.

Personally, I could rarely make out the backmasking messages, but just hearing a record backward really spooked me! The evangelical world even produced a series of videos called *Hell's Bells,* which featured former rock industry insiders revealing "what's really behind" rock, hip-hop, and rap artists and the music they produce. All this may have been productive, and I'm not saying that it wasn't. But when I started speaking on the issue of pornography, I wanted to avoid sounding like those guys who seemed to try to scare by unveiling a secret conspiracy. Maybe it can't be avoided.

Still, there is cause for great concern, especially with the growing alliance between porn and popular bands from the hip-hop, rock, and metal genres. They are representing a tour de force aimed at robbing young people of their innocence. Unfortunately, these music industry giants easily capture the imaginations of young fans. A writer for the Toronto *Star* notes how a band's relationship with the world of porn is a major factor in drawing a broader fan base: "The band Korn, for example, garnered early credibility among fans by posting interviews with porn stars on its Web site. The Insane Clown Posse goes on cable-access porn shows. Fred Durst appeared in *Backstage Sluts 2*. Porn gives bands cool points and boosts their fan base."[10] Wildly popular rapper Kanye West, who was exposed to porn at age 5 after finding his father's *Playboy* magazine, spoke publicly about his addiction and affection for pornography in a 2006 *Rolling Stone* article: "I have normal conversations all the time while I'm looking at these sites. . . . It's an addiction. Whenever we go to the porn store, we call it the crack house. I have porn on me at all times." West describes the first time he saw his father's *Playboy,* saying, "Right then [laughing] it was like, 'Houston, we have a problem.'"[11] Apparently West can't begin to understand the depths of the problem.

I'm certain that many young people are suffocating under the death grip of pornography and masturbation. If you're a young man or woman reading this book, I want to tell you that pornography isn't a joke, as some of your friends might like you to think. It certainly isn't part of God's plan for your sexuality, and you may not realize the damage it is doing. You might feel virtually unscathed by the occasional trip into pornland. But let me tell you that there will be many of you who won't be able to let it go—or rather it won't be able to let you go.

Stuck

I attended college in Texas, and rather than living in the dormitory, a couple guys and I rented a house across the street from the college campus—actually, it was directly across the street from the girls' dorm. The house was nothing special, but it did allow us the freedom to come and go as we liked without any dorm curfews. However, our little house had a severe mouse problem, and we were constantly trying to destroy the little creatures. (I'm sure the mice thought it was paradise since one of our roommates was rather fond of Domino's pizza and preserved the boxes for the valuable coupons attached to the top.)

Initially, we purchased traditional mousetraps. But after catching a few mice, we opted to try the more humane traps with a yellow, sticky, gellike substance designed to snag the mice as they scampered across them. Sure enough, the traps were quite effective, although I'd question whether or not they were actually more humane.

One day when I stopped by the house between classes, one of my roommates called me into the kitchen. He was standing near the sink with a bewildered look on his face, and there was a commotion from the cabinet underneath the sink where we had placed one of our sticky traps. Neither of us could imagine a little mouse making that much of a stir. So my roommate carefully opened the cabinet to discover not only a squealing mouse but also a live snake stuck to the sticky paper. In its attempt to devour the little mouse that had become easy prey on the trap, the snake became stuck to the trap as well.

Like the snake, it is easy to become a prisoner of our own cravings. Not only do we become broken, but like the snake, we become "stuck," too. The book of James gives a rather grim description of the same concept: "But each one is tempted when, by his own evil desire, he is *dragged away and enticed*. Then, after *de-*

sire has conceived, it gives birth to sin; and sin, when it is full-grown, gives birth to *death*" (James 1:14, 15). Neither the snake nor the mouse made it out of the house alive. Pornography has that effect on you. It hollows you out, leaving you but an empty shell, a dead corpse. To put it bluntly, pornography kills! It leaves you shallow and unable to fully relate to those around you.

---

[1] Pamela Paul, *Pornified,* pp. 49, 50.

[2] *Ibid.,* p. 67.

[3] www.toptenreviews.com.

[4] *Friends* sitcom episode "The One With the Free Porn," originally aired March 26, 1998.

[5] Dr. Judith Reisman, www.commerce.senate.gov/hearings.

[6] In Reisman, "Stimulating Images, Damaged Minds," www.worldnetdaily.com/news/article.asp?ARTICLE_ID=27896.

[7] Mark B. Kastleman, *The Drug of the New Millennium: The Brain Science Behind Internet Pornography Use: Three Power Principles Guaranteed to Protect Your Family* (2007), chap. 3.

[8] Laurie Hall, *An Affair of the Mind,* p. 100.

[9] www.toptenreviews.com.

[10] R. J. Smith, "Rap Metal Mooks," Toronto *Star,* Aug. 15, 2000.

[11] *Rolling Stone,* Feb. 9, 2006.

Chapter 11

WAGING A SUCCESSFUL BATTLE

"For our struggle is not against flesh and blood, but against the rulers, against the authorities, against the powers of this dark world and against the spiritual forces of evil in the heavenly realms."—Ephesians 6:12.

"Be very careful, then, how you live—not as unwise but as wise, making the most of every opportunity, because the days are evil."—Ephesians 5:15, 16.

During the summers I spent working as a staff member at camp, there was one sound that always got my adrenaline pumping: the drag siren screaming from the swimming area. It was a high-decibel, emergency, whooping sound that was transported throughout the camp by strategically placed speakers. The shrill scream of the drag siren told the staff that during one of the regularly scheduled waterfront buddy checks a camper was unaccounted for and presumed to be in the water—which meant that we had very little time to get to them. It also meant that a search or drag must be done at once. It didn't matter where you were or what you were doing—at the sound of that siren staff members had to make a beeline for the swimming area.

The procedure for a drag required a diver with scuba gear to search the deepest part of the designated swimming area while the rest of the staff formed a human chain in the shallow end, working their way down into deeper water. Hooked arm and arm, we carefully walked through every inch of the area. It was always a bit unnerving, feeling our way along the muddy bottom of the lake with our feet. Looking down into the murky water, we hoped that the child simply forgot to check out and was back at their cabin slipping into some dry clothes. This was life or death. A child was missing. To lose someone at summer camp would be devastating.

Tragically there are many Christians drowning in the depths of pornography. Who knows where it started—maybe curiosity simply got the best of them. But curiosity has led to an overwhelming obsession keeping them from breaking out of the dark place they're in. The goal of this book is not only to share my personal story but to sound the alarm, alerting everyone to the fact that pornography is taking a toll on the church—especially the men in our church.

Have you ever wondered why there are far more women in church than there are men? Ever wondered why women are often the ones carrying the load of ministry? Even when we guys are involved, it seems to be at a minimal level. A statement from Ken Luck of Every Man Ministries indicates that guys recognize that pornography is a major hindrance to their spiritual walk: "Nine out of 10 of the 500 men attending a church retreat in California indicated that lust, porn, and fantasy were the habitual, continual, or fatal disconnecting factors in their relationship with God."

If pornography is hindering the spiritual walk of many men, it's likely a significant barrier to fully embracing a call to serve in the local church. No, I'm not suggesting that every guy in our churches is so guilt-ridden over a problem with lust that he resists involvement in church. What I am saying is that hidden sin of any type essentially renders us spiritually feeble, unable to live out our mission in an authentic way. So rather than run the risk of being seen as a fake or hypocrite, most will opt out and choose to remain at a distance from God and the church rather than seek direction and guidance.

But sin doesn't have to keep men on the run and hiding from God. Since there aren't any perfect Christians, we need to send the message to men that most Christians lead with a limp. We're all on a journey, fully dependent upon God's grace and mercy.

Spiritual Motivation

Spiritual motivation is a key factor in gaining freedom from the tyranny of pornography. It isn't enough to simply *want* to be free from the disruption that lust brings to your life; there has to be a bigger purpose in mind. That purpose should stem from an understanding that God is able to fulfill the deepest longings of your soul. Sexual desire is a good thing. God has given us something good, and it's meant for our pleasure. But that which God has created for our good can easily become the thing we illegitimately rely upon to comfort or distract us when life gets challenging.

Rather than worshipping God and having our needs legitimately met by the One who said "Come to me . . . and I will give you rest" (Matthew 11:28), it's easy to begin to worship that which God has created. As C. S. Lewis talks about in several of his books, including *The Four Loves,* love—and eros, or sexual love—will cease to be a demon when it ceases to be a god. When we take sex off the altar of our hearts and restore God as the focus of our worship, then the gift of sexual fulfillment can be experienced in the context that God intended. To be spiritually motivated to break the bondage of porn is to seek to worship the Creator rather than that which He created.

BRIDGE: God's Way to Initiate Change

To have a practical biblical process that diminishes porn's stronghold is essential to rescuing those who have fallen into the trap of choosing porn over purity. I've developed an acrostic, BRIDGE, to help illustrate what I believe is God's way of initiating and bringing about transformation in a man's life.

Brokenness

"For You do not desire sacrifice, or else I would give it; You do not delight in burnt offering. The sacrifices of God are a broken spirit, a broken and a contrite heart" (Psalm 51:16, 17, NKJV).

"When I kept silent, my bones wasted away through my groaning all day long" (Psalm 32:3).

I believe that brokenness is the launching pad for God's work of transformation. When we arrive at this point (through the Holy Spirit), we are vulnerable, teachable, and humble. This is where we begin to gain an understanding for God's utter abhorrence of our sin problem. Most men don't arrive at this point until they've gone to the depths of sexual sin or have lost the things that are most important to them, such as a family, job, home, or money.

Two things are important about brokenness. First, it will be a major indicator of how serious you are about making a change. If it is real, then there will be a deep desire to submit to the Holy Spirit's leading and the leading of other men in seeking out help and recovery. Second, there will be an inner truth crisis—you'll come to see the double life you've been leading and will desire wholeness and integrity more than anything else. These desires become your driving forces, leading you from brokenness to wholeness. Brokenness indicates real sorrow for sin, such as what King David demonstrated after being confronted by the prophet Nathan. Brokenness is a work of God's Spirit. If you find yourself longing for change, even praying earnestly for God to change your heart, it's an indication that perhaps God is moving you toward brokenness, through which He will restore you.

Repentance

"Godly sorrow brings *repentance* that leads to salvation and leaves no regret, but worldly sorrow brings death" (2 Corinthians 7:10).

"Truly, these times of ignorance God overlooked, but now commands all men everywhere to repent" (Acts 17:30, NKJV).

The next part in God's process of setting us free is repentance. Out of our sorrow and desire to change comes an actual turning away from what holds us in bondage. It isn't just avoiding porn. It's intentionally turning away and seeking something new and pure—returning to God as the prodigal returned to the father. Repentance is an act of submission toward God and His will for our lives.

Repentance won't be a onetime event for a guy attempting to kick a porn habit; it will become a regular spiritual discipline. Real repentance finds substance in actions. That's why Matthew 3:8 says, "Produce fruit in keeping with repentance." Real repentance won't just express sorrow for sin. It will demonstrate an actual change in direction that will be obvious not only to you but to others.

Involvement

"Therefore, my dear friends, as you have always obeyed—not only in my presence, but now much more in my absence—continue to work out your salvation with fear and trembling, for it is God who works in you to will and to act according to his good purpose" (Philippians 2:12, 13).

"Fight the good fight of the faith. Take hold of the eternal life to which you were called when you made your good confession in the presence of many witnesses" (1 Timothy 6:12).

Passivity is the anchor that keeps many chained to pornography. Significant change through God's Spirit happens with intentionality. A man arranges his life in such a way that his activities demonstrate that he desires to honor God with his body. Voluntarily joining a men's accountability group, seeking out a pastor or spiritual advisor, or employing a licensed counselor all reveal that a man is interested in dealing with this problem. A man intent on living with integrity in this area will change his TV viewing habits and guard the avenues to the soul very carefully. It may even mean that he gives up watching Sunday football altogether because of the sexy cheerleaders. While his natural tendency is to be passive about sexual purity, he'll become pro-active in his pursuit of sexual integrity. His attitude will change. A man seeking God's direction will display a humble spirit as he involves himself in God's process of change.

Discipline

"No discipline seems pleasant at the time, but painful. Later on, however, it produces a harvest of righteousness and peace for those who have been trained by it" (Hebrews 12:11).

"For God did not give us a spirit of timidity, but a spirit of power, of love and of self-discipline" (2 Timothy 1:7).

"Rather he must be hospitable, one who loves what is good, who is self-controlled, upright, holy and disciplined" (Titus 1:8).

Discipline can't be seen as merely punishment for a serious wrongdoing. Discipline is meant to teach, guide, and correct for the sake of restoration. It can be said that no real change ever comes without discipline. Again, a spirit of submission is required on the part of a man receiving discipline. The word discipline is derived from the word "disciple." In the New Testament the word disciple in Greek is *matheteis*, which means "learner." A man comes under the tutelage of the Holy Spirit when he experiences discipline. Therefore he must see himself as a learner or disciple. The goal of the teacher is to pass along instruction so that the man can experience the best of this life and not be brought down because he's not guided. This is the role of a good father, because he loves his children deeply. Correction through discipline teaches us consistency, while providing insight through the wisdom of God's Spirit and others God involves in the process.

Grace

"From the fullness of his grace we have all received one blessing after another" (John 1:16). "The law was added so that the trespass might increase. But where sin increased, grace increased all the more" (Romans 5:20). "But he said to me, 'My grace is sufficient for you, for my power is made perfect in weakness.' Therefore I will boast all the more gladly about my weaknesses, so that Christ's power may rest on me" (2 Corinthians 12:9).

The role of grace in the process of turnaround cannot be understated. Grace is a catalyst to change, not a license for indulgence. I'm very bothered when some people claim that the message of grace creates lazy Christians who really aren't concerned about personal holiness. It's knowing that you're loved, adopted, and secure that compels you to act in a loving, obedient, and holy manner. To revere God's holiness comes from experiencing a new birth and conversion. This may be initiated by realizing that you're in direct opposition to God's law (which reflects His will and character), but what sustains the believer over the long haul is a relationship based on love and freedom. This relationship then serves as the catalyst to authentic and deep personal change through the influence of the Holy Spirit.

Grace must also be seen as a period for repentance. Author Joe Dallas calls this "space for repentance" and describes how we tend to react to this grace space: "If you've been given space to repent, you'll do one of two things: you'll either use it wisely by taking action while you can, or you'll make the common mistake of mistaking space for repentance as permission to continue. That's easy to do, because we tend to be consequence-driven. When we get away with something once, we're inclined to think we'll get away with it indefinitely."[1] God doesn't take pleasure in our embarrassment or the ripping apart of our family. He would rather see us change before things turn ugly.

Endurance

"Therefore, since we are surrounded by such a great cloud of witnesses, let us throw off everything that hinders and the sin that so easily entangles, and let us run with perseverance the race marked out for us" (Hebrews 12:1).

"Being strengthened with all power according to his glorious might so that you may have great endurance and patience" (Colossians 1:11).

"For everything that was written in the past was written to teach us, so that through endurance and the encouragement of the Scriptures we might have hope" (Romans 15:4).

We've often heard the saying that life is really a marathon and not a sprint. That is the case with traveling the path toward sexual purity. It's carried out over the long haul and demands endurance. It isn't a white-knuckle experience, either. Not in the sense that you are constantly on the verge of giving in to lust and pornography. What we do hang on to with everything we've got is Jesus and His promises, guidance, and direction. The Holy Spirit becomes our coach as we attempt to make our way in this race. Others will be needed as well to provide encouragement and support. There will need to be times of rest and reflection.

That is why devotional, prayer, and Bible study times, as well as Sabbath rest, are so important. These disciplines for the believer build endurance and stamina to meet the challenges of this life. I would suggest that we carry Sabbath moments over into the rest of our week as well. Let's not confine the rest and worship we experience just to Friday night and Saturday! It isn't healthy during the week to wear ourselves out to the point that, when Sabbath arrives, we can hardly function on a spiritual or physical level. Light moments of recreation and play throughout the week are healing oil and provide a necessary outlet. We can't become so serious that we forget how to play. Our goal is to experience life in all its fullness without letting sin dictate how we will live.

Porn—the Enemy of Intimacy

Most men and women who struggle with porn would agree that pornography is an enemy of intimacy. If porn is an ongoing struggle for you, then it has also disconnected you from the people around you. Some experts even say that pornography addiction is an actual *intimacy disorder*. To create intimacy, then, is essential to combat the lure of pornography. To create intimacy, though, demands that we take the focus off ourselves and begin to invest in those around us. Pornography turns us inward, isolating us like a hermit crab in a shell. The shell we enjoy not only shelters us from pain, but it cheats us, family, and friends out of the relationship we were meant to have.

In general, this is the scariest part for us men. I know it has been for me. Of all the things I've done in this life, none frightens me more than allowing those closest to me to know who I am. That sounds strange because you would like to think that simply by living together long enough you would know a person. But that isn't always the case. To create intimacy we have to be willing and courageous enough to honestly tell our story—not just our stories of failure and sin, but the story of our lives. Intimacy is to trust our spouse with the most intimate details of our past. But sharing on this level makes us vulnerable. And yes, we run the risk of pain and devastation. Yet that is simply a risk we must take. One of the best things a married man can do is sit down with his wife and have a deep conversation in which he tells her who he is—his past, present, hopes, dreams, fears, and desires for the future. Here are some practical ideas for how you can begin to open your life up to your wife and significant others.

- *Set up a talk date.* Find a secluded place where you can both be comfortable taking turns telling each other the story of your lives.
- *Write letters.* It's a lost art that needs to make a comeback. You may find your words better by putting them down on paper. Rather than letting your spouse just read it alone, read it aloud to her or him. If you need help, check out www.lettersfromdad.com.
- *Create a video message.* Set up the camera and just talk away as if your wife were sitting there in front of you. Then make a date to watch it together.
- *Limit media consumption.* This is half the battle. Simply by turning things off, we eliminate some major distractions that prevent us from authentically connecting to real people. Unplug!
- *Listen.* James says to be "quick to listen, slow to speak" (James 1:19). That is so important in creating intimacy. But you have to really listen with both your ears and your heart.

Getting Accountable

Like two center tent poles, intimacy and accountability are essential to upholding any commitment you make to sexual integrity. I can't emphasize enough how important accountability is for every man and woman (especially for pastors). To be accountable is to have to answer to someone rather than acting autonomously. Accountability is effective, though, only if the person desiring accountability earnestly seeks to achieve a certain result. For example, I've had some accountability with this book. It has been a stated goal of mine to complete this project before I'm so old that I can't see a computer screen. I knew it would be a major undertaking considering the schedule that I keep. Yet I've had this on my heart to do. Left to myself, however, I would likely fiddle around with it and never really get anywhere. But in this case I've had people speaking into my life, encouraging me, asking me, "Have you written another chapter?" So there was really no way around it if I was going to be a man of my word.

The same is true for any aspect of our lives, especially for living with integrity in the sexual arena. In this case there must be a person or people we can be downright honest with on a regular basis—someone who won't accept our fluffy, pretentious answers that we try to pass off as truth in order to avoid the pain of honesty. For guys struggling with porn, I do *not* recommend your wife as your primary accountability partner. There is automatically some accountability with her simply because you are married, but she didn't sign up for that as a career—and it isn't fair to ask her to live on the roller coaster of our inconsistency in the area of sexual purity. You should prayerfully seek out another man—someone whom you respect and who will truly hold you to the accountability that you need.

Masturbation

As a youth pastor I enjoyed taking a group of my students on a rafting trip every year on the Brazos River in New Braunfels, Texas. It had been our practice to stay at the home of a wonderful Christian couple who very generously opened their house to our group. But one year their home was not available, so we had to look for an alternative that was not only cheap, but appropriate for our coed group. We ended up sleeping at a local church. We segregated the group, sending the girls inside to sleep on the classroom floors, with many of the guys opting to sleep outside under the stars.

On trips such as this, the students generally took awhile to wind down and drift off to sleep. So one of the male sponsors and I milled around outside talking with the guys as they were settling into their sleeping bags. The male sponsor caught me a little off guard when he laughingly said, "There will be no tent building tonight, guys!" I had never heard that expression before, but I soon caught on to its meaning. He was talking about that taboo "M" word—masturbation. It's something that many people do, but no one ever talks about, especially among church people.

In 1991 Bart Campolo, the son of the fiery Tony Campolo, wrote an article that he entitled "Three Things My Youth Leader Never Told Me About Masturbation." Bart called it "an open letter to junior high leaders about a secret, silent struggle almost all kids face."

I have had this article filed away since I came across it back in 1995, at a time when masturbation was an ongoing source of spiritual anguish for me. I was confused about whether or not it was a sin. But no one ever talked about it. The only time I heard anything was in a joke or when someone referenced Ellen White writing about the detrimental physical affects of self-abuse, which I ultimately learned referred to masturbation. But since pornography and masturbation are coconspirators in undermining our attempts at purity, we have to openly talk about how we can best deal with these two issues. By addressing the issue of masturbation, I hope I can help those who are just as confused as I was.

In his book *The Sexual Man*, Dr. Archibald Hart gives the results of a survey of some 600 Christian men on the topic of masturbation:

61 percent of married Christian men masturbate (have self sex);

82 percent of these men have self sex on an average of once a week;

10 percent have sex with self 5 to 10 times per month;

6 percent do it more than 15 times per month;

1 percent do it more than 20 times a month;

13 percent of Christian married men said they felt it was normal.[2]

Clearly, Christian men are dealing with this issue, and the question I'm often asked about masturbation is whether or not it is a sinful act. To answer that question, some refer to the Old Testament story of Onan. Onan was the second son of Judah who eventually married Tamar. According to Hebrew law, after the death of Onan's brother Er, Onan was required to take Tamar (Er's widow) as his wife. The firstborn child of the couple would be considered Er's heir. According to Genesis 38:9, 10, when having sexual intercourse with his wife Tamar, Onan "spilled his semen on the ground" and as a result was put to death by God.

The interpretation has been that Onan masturbated, and since he was met with such punishment, this must demonstrate a prohibition against masturbation. But a more accurate interpretation would reveal that Onan's actions represented his refusal to follow divine law. Disgruntled over having to father a child who wouldn't be considered his, Onan used the "pullout" method of contraception so he wouldn't impregnate his wife Tamar. We can interpret the severe punishment he incurred as a judgment against his attempt to skirt his obligations and responsibilities under the law.

The Bible seems to support the notion that we men are visually stimulated. Remember the warning Jesus gave that's recorded in Matthew 5:28: "But I tell you that anyone who looks at a woman lustfully has already committed adultery with her in his heart." With that understanding, as men we are in somewhat of a catch-22, since we live in a culture in which at every turn we are invited to take in potentially dangerous images. Our minds can easily convert them into sexual fantasies that are drawn upon the instant the sexual urge arises. Since we can't walk around wearing blindfolds, we have to learn how to properly respond to our environment. It will require a change of heart and mind (Romans 12:1 and Psalm 51:10, 11). Rather than objectifying a woman with ogling glances and stares, we have to learn to see a woman's beauty as God's creative handiwork and leave it at that.

Granted, it is difficult to know when you've crossed the line from appreciating the God-given beauty of a woman (or man) to recording images to your brain's hard drive for easy access at a later time. So we must constantly remind ourselves that our sexual fulfillment was meant for only our wives or husbands, and that God deems sinful any sexual activity outside of the marital relationship, even if we're just "looking."

It's natural to have the urge for sexual release through masturbation. Even though our bodies as males naturally release semen through nocturnal emissions, it seems as though our fires are perpetually burning. But just because it's natural doesn't mean it's always right. Paul indicated that eating is healthy because food was made for the stomach. But Paul never endorses overeating, or making a god out of food. Paul writes that people say, "'Food for the stomach and the stomach for food'—but God will destroy them both. The body is not meant for sexual immorality, but for the Lord, and the Lord for the body" (1 Corinthians 6:13).

We have to understand that masturbation is sex with self, which is directly at odds with what God intended for the sexual experience. Joshua Harris puts it this way in his book *Sex Is Not the Problem (Lust Is)*, formerly entitled *Not Even a Hint*: "Masturbation is built on a self-centered view of sex. This wrong attitude says that sex is solely about you and your pleasure. Your body. Your genitals. Your orgasm. This is the natural tendency of sin. It isolates us from others and makes pleasure self-focused. When our lustful desires are given free rein, sex is pushed into a corner and made a completely self-centered, isolated experience that reinforces a self-centered view of life."[3]

Curb the Urge

To be successful at curbing the urge to masturbate, two things are important: (1) recognize when you're vulnerable, and (2) know what triggers your forays. Armed with this knowledge, you can incorporate activities to replace the default setting of simply giving in to masturbation.

Recognize vulnerable times:
- Experiencing feelings of stress, fear, rejection, abandonment
- Taking long, hot showers
- Watching late-night TV
- Being in a private office
- Being in hotel rooms
- Surfing the Internet when alone
- Thumbing through magazines at a bookstore

- Feeling **H**ungry, **A**ngry, **L**onely, **T**ired (HALT!)
- Channel surfing

Recognize common triggers:
- Billboards
- Innocent people-watching (airport, mall, church)
- Joggers
- Fitness centers
- Beach
- Sunday ads/lingerie ads/Victoria's Secret catalogs
- Magazine racks at the checkout counters in the grocery store
- Provocative or sexually oriented news stories (online or on TV)
- Social networking sites (MySpace, Facebook, etc.)
- Photo-sharing sites

This is by no means an exhaustive list. The point is to know when you are vulnerable, and then know the things that trigger the acting out. Learn to keep your head about you and respond appropriately to situations in which you're stimulated and tempted. How we respond to the situation will make the difference as to whether or not we're successful in the battle. If we react in our normal way (often emotionally driven—it feels good, so I'll go with it), we'll lose every time. But if we respond to the Holy Spirit, we're more likely to find success. "So I say, live by the Spirit, and you will not gratify the desires of the sinful nature" (Galatians 5:16). Eventually those strongholds that have held ground for so long begin to break away, diminishing their power to control us.

After reading this chapter, you may be left wondering where the secret formula for freedom is. I've offered some suggestions and de-scribed what I think is God's process for reclaiming you. You'll find some strategies to implement, but I haven't offered a magic pill or fast track to be rid of porn forever. There really is no formula, no magic pill, nothing that can cure you in an instant. You must em-bark on a journey. You must be willing to travel a path that you've resisted far too long. My goal has been to let you know that there is such a path. Yes, it will demand much of you. But you won't be alone, because your Savior and King promises to guide you along the way. He just asks that you trust Him.

[1] J. Dallas, *The Game Plan*, p. 20.
[2] Archibald Hart, *The Sexual Man*, pp. 136-139.
[3] Joshua Harris, *Sex Is Not the Problem (Lust Is)*, p. 103.

Chapter 12

PASTOR TO PASTOR

"For physical training is of some value, but godliness has value for all things, holding promise for both the present life and the life to come."—1 Timothy 4:8.

"Watch your life and doctrine closely. Persevere in them, because if you do, you will save both yourself and your hearers."—1 Timothy 4:16.

I live in a region of the United States where in the wintertime the snow piles high on the mountains and ski resorts teem with people out to have a good time on the slopes. But there's another group, usually locals, who are more daring than others. They have no interest in the well-groomed, sterile resort scene. These adventure seekers travel into the backcountry in search of pure, untouched, powdery terrain. The backcountry is wide-open, free of recreational types, and tests the skills of anyone willing to venture out. But the backcountry is also deadly. The real danger in the backcountry is that you could trigger an avalanche—an enormous wave of snow that can overtake you, turning your backcountry excursion into a desperate fight for survival. Skiing outside the boundaries is a wild, unpredictable journey in which you ski at your own risk. The posted signs are clear: "You could die!"

Ask most any pastor, and they'll tell you that ministry resembles the treacherous adventure of skiing the backcountry. Ministry is unpredictable, wild, and downright scary at times. Now, we did sign up for it; we willingly ventured into unknown terrain, but apparently we forgot to read the sign carefully: "Danger—enter ministry at your own risk!" It was meant to be that way, though. To carry out the work of the Master is to invite discomfort. Jesus never attempted to gloss over the potential hazards of leading the life of a disciple. In Luke 9 we read of Jesus' encounter with an enthusiastic volunteer who proclaimed that he was ready to follow Jesus wherever He went. Somewhere, apparently, the zealous recruit got the impression that this was the thing to do, some sort of new fad. Jesus received a lot of attention, and perhaps he thought it might be beneficial to ride the bandwagon for a while. Jesus returned a rather sobering message: "Foxes have holes and birds of the air have nests, but the Son of Man has no place to lay his head" (Luke 9:58).

Essentially Jesus is saying, "Do you really know what you're asking? Forget everything you've been told about what it means to follow Me, because you've been given the wrong impression. To follow Me is to risk everything—it may even mean not having a place to sleep at night."

If you're a pastor, you know as well as I do that the dangers in the backcountry of ministry are real. For many of us, an avalanche of things has already broken free, and our experience in ministry is to scramble to stay ahead and keep from being overwhelmed. Our calendars are full—so are our stomachs—but our hearts are weighed down. We find ourselves vulnerable to most anything that's safe and warm. Yet our call is real. When Jesus said, "Come follow Me," we did (see Matthew 4:19). And though we find ourselves saying, "They didn't teach us that in seminary!" we're still God's men and women right now in the place where He's called us.

To navigate the ever-changing landscape of ministry requires a skilled guide, one who knows the backcountry well. Jesus has traveled the uncomfortable path, so we can look to Him for guidance. Returning to the story in Luke 9, we see Jesus setting out on what will be His last journey to Jerusalem. Back in verse 51, Luke says that He set out "resolutely" toward Jerusalem. In other words, He put His mind to the journey ahead without wavering, unlike His potential followers, who suddenly had other priorities, such as burying a dead relative and saying goodbye to family.

Jesus had clarity about His calling, and even knowing what lay ahead, He willingly set out. Clarity is important for us pastors, too. Clarity breeds purpose, meaning, direction. Have you asked yourself lately what you're supposed to be doing beyond the safety of shepherding your people? Are you afraid to disrupt the status quo and so never attempt anything new? Maybe you're like me, with a tendency toward attempting only the things that I have a fairly good chance of pulling off. That way I'm guaranteed at least moderate success. I've often settled for the more tame terrain rather than risk injury or looking like a fool on some new adventure.

But playing it safe won't sustain us over the long haul. We have to return to our younger years, when we approached ministry with reckless abandon. Our eyes were wide open; we hungered for adventure—to do something big for the kingdom of God. Our preaching was risky, passionate, original. It wasn't that we were trying to build the next megachurch or become a best-selling Christian author. We weren't in it for the celebrity or potential fortune. It was the journey that lured us, a journey into the unknown. The rewards were seeing the fruit produced by the Spirit of God. To see hearts, once dimmed by the stain of sin, miraculously come back to life renewed and hopeful. Have I made my point? Pastor, the backcountry is where you belong.

So, right now, jettison any notion of ditching ministry. Trust me—I've been there many times. My wife knows when I'm getting antsy. It's when I reach for the employment ads in the Sunday paper, wondering if there's some job out there that will take a guy with a theology degree! If I could just make more money, live in a better house, drive a nicer car—that would be the life. It's a lot more appealing than the worship wars, potlucks, and board meetings. But you know as well as I do that we'd still be discontented.

You may think I've strayed from the purpose of this chapter—chasing a rabbit, as we call it in preaching. You were looking for the typical "don't counsel a female member alone behind closed doors" and "meet with an accountability partner regularly." These are important measures to take (and I do talk about them later), but that isn't where we begin. You see, pornography is simply a way to hide the fear of entering the backcountry. It's a refusal to live in the fullness of God's Spirit, which was implanted in us at conversion. When we've lost a courageous heart, pornography is the ultimate distraction. All the accountability strategies, Internet filters, and counseling won't help a pastor who won't follow his or her calling to enter the backcountry.

A New Call

Often the opportunity for new adventure comes along at awkward times and from the must unlikeliest places. That was the case in 2004 when I received a call from the head elder of a church in Salt Lake City, Utah. He had received my name and phone number from another pastor friend of mine, and called to see if I had any interest in coming to pastor his church. He also inquired about my story and where things were with my recovery. I let him know that things were going well and while the idea of leading only one congregation was attractive I wasn't sure that Salt Lake City was the place for my family or me. In the back of my mind I figured that once this church got a hold of the *Newsweek* article that would be the end of any interest in me anyway. We weren't being pushed out of our churches and I wanted to stay and continue to minister to the congregations that had been impacted by my failure.

Besides Christina and I wanted to remain in Texas close to my mother and the many friendships we had gained over the years. But the church in Salt Lake City was very much interested in us and, as it would turn out, we had already planned a family vacation to Zion National Park in southern Utah. I let the elder of the church know that we would be in Utah and I told him that I would be willing to come and speak during my vacation. I thought for sure it wouldn't go well and that would be the end of any potential call to Utah. Things went well, however, and Christina and I were well received by the congregation. We eventually went through a formal interview process with the local church and conference leadership.

Obviously the issue of my past porn problem came up during all of this and while I'm sure it was a problem for some the conference still extended an invitation.

Christina and I were still not convinced that it was the move to make. For me, I wasn't sure if I wanted to pull Christina away from the familiar surroundings of close friends and the support network she had in Texas. Since I had already caused such pain I was hesitant to inflict more trauma with a major move. And so, after much contemplation and prayer, we decided to decline the invitation. However the elder who initially contacted us was incredibly persistent, believing that we were the team that needed to come to his church. Through our conversations he and I had forged an instant friendship, and I felt like he sincerely cared for my family and that our ministry would be well received by his church. So Christina and I reconsidered and eventually accepted the call to Utah.

Now we were in a new church, new city, culture, and environment. People in the area knew about my story but I sensed that Christina appreciated a bit of anonymity in moving to a different city. But it was short-lived. During our first year in Utah I got a call from Craig Gross, the cofounder of www.xxxchurch.com, a ministry that regularly pushes the envelope in their efforts to help guys kick the porn problem. Their latest project was called Porn Sunday, and ABC News wanted to do a story.

Craig asked if I would be willing to be a part. Since the story would air nationally on a major network evening news program I followed the same routine I had in Texas by first approaching Christina about the invitation. Once she gave her blessing I called my conference president. My conference president called other leaders. They were all in agreement that I should go forward with the interview. The move to Utah wasn't really a part of our plans, but that is the nature of ministry. We aren't always clear where God will call us.

Fearful Tendencies

The story is told that boxing great Muhammad Ali was seated on a plane when a flight attendant asked him to buckle up for takeoff.

The champ responded with one of his notorious, witty comments, saying, "Supaman don't need no seat belt!"

"Supaman don't need no *plane!*" the flight attendant quipped back.

Sometimes members view us pastors as superhuman. And while we may not come right out and say it, at times we've demonstrated an air of invincibility, choosing to navigate the rigors of ministry like some caped superhero.

Most pastors are hard workers, committing a vast number of hours to study, ministry to their people, and to special projects, yet often neglecting any personal care. Couple that with the pressures of family, finances, and living in a fishbowl, and you've got a recipe for vulnerability to almost anything that provides an easy getaway. A closer, honest look would also reveal that we pastors battle an overwhelming sense of inadequacy and insecurity. I know that at times I've found myself depressed after encountering a member's negative comment, or I've allowed myself to overanalyze an innocent joke from a lighthearted conversation with a member.

Add to these the frequent episodes of paranoia related to whether or not I'm accepted and loved by my congregation. Loneliness tends to be rampant among us pastors as well. I'll confess that this has been one of my ongoing sources of anxiety over the years. To combat this I've had to be intentional about spending time with others and not allowing myself to become isolated in my own secluded ministry bubble.

Another unhealthy tendency I've displayed as a pastor is to be a people pleaser. I would rather spend most of my ministry avoiding the awkwardness of confrontation and get on with the business of introducing people to a relationship with Jesus. But to avoid confrontation is to avoid intimacy. To act as if everything is OK when things aren't is to lie, and it leads to inauthentic and toxic relationships. What I've found is that healthy pastors and healthy congregations are able to confront in an appropriate Christlike way. This allows both groups to know where they stand. Pastors who are people pleasers will often suppress their true feelings so they won't disappoint their members. Eventually, those things that have been internalized have to find an outlet somewhere, and that is where pornography becomes a willing partner.

But it isn't just the challenges of ministry or the emotional stress that can lead to disaster. You know as well as I do the seductive nature of success and the intoxicating effect of a compliment. In my own battle with pornography, some of my most vulnerable times were when I experienced success in ministry. Perhaps subconsciously we start believing in too many of the good things members tell us about our sermons, demonstrations of compassion, and biblical insights. Whatever the case, don't be surprised at the subtle lure that accomplishment and accolades can bring. These lead to a sense of entitlement; they lead us to act as though we can do or have whatever we want.

The Dark Side of Leadership

At least five ancient Greek philosophers are credited with having coined the phrase "Know thyself." It's important advice for pastors and church leaders. Like anyone else, those of us called to service on behalf of God's kingdom enter ministry with a darkness that, if not dealt with appropriately, can be our undoing. In their excellent book *Overcoming the Dark Side of Leadership,* authors Gary McIntosh and Samuel Rima explain: "The dark side, though sounding quite sinister, is actually a natural result of human development. It is the inner urges, compulsions, and dysfunctions of our personality that often go unexamined or remain unknown to us until we experience an emotional explosion."[1]

McIntosh and Rima are describing the inner drivenness that each leader/pastor possesses with the inference that our examination of those shadowy sides helps prevent compromise.

The authors further describe the nature of our dark side: "Like vinegar and soda being slowly swirled together in a tightly closed container, our personalities have been slowly intermingled with examples, emotions, expectations, and experiences that over a lifetime have created our dark side."[2]

It's vitally important for us as pastors and church leaders to carefully examine our lives. We need to come to terms with the lurking shadows that threaten our ministries. I think at some level we all recognize that there is a dark side to us. It's just difficult to look at and even more frightening to honestly confront. Yet we must confront it if we're to be effective ministers. We must consider who we are at the deepest level, what's motivating us, and what we are most vulnerable to.

Getting Accountable

It demands some intentionality on our part, but the inconvenience we might feel from meeting with someone weekly for accountability and implementing real boundaries is nothing compared to the potential damage to the name of Christ (*and* our families) that could come as a result of a public sexual fall. It is well-known that over the course of his long ministry evangelist Billy Graham has had some significant accountability practices in place. Not being in a room alone with a woman and not even staying in a hotel room next door to a single female are safeguards he has stood by for years. Pastor Rick Warren (Saddleback Community Church) has 10 commandments for sexual integrity that he and his staff live by. Pastor Mark Driscoll (Mars Hill Church, Seattle) screens everything, including mail, e-mail, and phone calls, through a male assistant.

While some might think such measures are a bit radical and unwarranted, Scripture admonishes you to "guard" what has been entrusted to your care," including your heart (1 Timothy 6:20). Paul encourages Timothy to "watch your life and ministry closely" (1 Timothy 4:16). It would be naive, even foolish, for us as leaders to engage in ministry without guarding against the attacks of our enemy. Here are some practical accountability structures that pastors can implement, whether they struggle to maintain sexual integrity or not.

Traveling and hotel rooms:

• When traveling alone (avoid it if you can), have the television removed from your room or the cable/satellite television totally turned off.

• Take books to read instead of watching the television (which leads to channel surfing, which leads to places you shouldn't be going).

• If the television temptation is just too much, then stay with church members when you travel. I know that it's a pain, but it might be necessary.

Online:

• Have software on your computer that keeps you accountable while surfing the Web. (x3watch from www.xxxchurch.com is a good one.)

• If you have to go online while on the road, call or e-mail an accountability partner letting them know that you are going on, what sites you are going to, and how long you will be on. When you are finished, call or e-mail them back to check in.

• Have e-mails screened through your secretary or wife. Don't let anyone have direct access to you through e-mail. Don't keep any e-mail account secret from your spouse. Make sure she has all user names and passwords to your e-mail accounts.

At church:

• Do not counsel alone with a member of the opposite sex. (Refer after two appointments.)

• Do not share a ride with someone of the opposite sex.

• Do not go out to eat (even if it is ministry-related) alone with the opposite sex.

• Your church office should have a window big enough that anyone can see what's going on inside.

• Let your wife's intuition be a guide when you interact with female members.

A PEACE Plan

An acrostic that may be helpful as pastors strive for balance in ministry is what I call the PEACE plan. It would be difficult, if not impossible, to carry out ministry in a constant state of turmoil or paranoia. Neither is there peace where there is hidden sexual sin. As an author and spouse of a pastor, Mary Southerland says, "We need to regularly expose and eliminate the 'mire' or sin in our lives since peace is always realized in a right relationship with God."[3]

• *Pursue*. Pursue sexual integrity every day. Proactively engage in activities that guard against any impurity that might pull you toward seeking an illegitimate way of dealing with pain, disappointment, and success. (See Philippians 4:8.)

• *Examine*. Examine your life regularly and submit to the scrutiny of others who support your ministry and want to see you grow. Remember what Socrates said: "The unexamined life is not worth living." (Also pray Psalm 26:1-3.)

• *Acknowledge*: Acknowledge your vulnerabilities as well as sinful activity. Through confession to an accountability partner and in private to God, acknowledge that you are under the constant care of the Holy Spirit who is doing a work of restoration in your life. Determine to live a life characterized by an awareness of who you are as God's child, and refute any claims Satan makes on your life. (Read Psalm 51:2-4 and Psalm 32:5.)

• *Care*: Submit to care from others at times. Care for your body through proper rest and regular exercise. Care for your mind through wholesome study, carefully guarding the avenues to the soul. Care for your family through spending quality time with them in real conversation and play. (Study Galatians 6:2; 2 Corinthians 1:3-7; and 1 John 4:21.)

• *Enlist*: Don't go it alone. Enlist the help of others as guides, mentors, and counselors. Whenever you're weak, be courageous enough to recruit the support of another, acknowledging the fact that you don't have all the answers and that the ministry is better carried out with a team than by a Lone Ranger—who wasn't really ever alone. He had Tonto! (See Hebrews 10:24; Galatians 6:1, 2; and Ecclesiastes 4:9, 10.)

Obviously more could be said, but I think the point is clear. If your ministry is teetering on the brink of disaster, then let me urge you to seek out help. So much debate has gone on about how to deal with the fallout of a pastor's moral failure. Even greater debate goes on about how to appropriately restore pastors to ministry once they've fallen sexually. I even had a colleague suggest that I devote a chapter to a procedure to deal with such situations. But honestly I'm not sure of the best way to handle it. Although I do hope that churches have well-thought-out plans that can be implemented in a crisis, my purpose here is to show you how to prevent the fall from occurring in the first place. It may be that you've gone along in ministry without any safeguards and done fine. But I'll tell you, you're living with a false sense of security, because the very nature of ministry in the backcountry warrants real vigilance when it comes to sexual integrity.

Some have and will continue to raise the question of discipline in my case. Why wasn't I immediately removed from my position as a pastor or put under some sort of mandatory leave or disciplinary action? Personally, I expected something to happen and was fully prepared to submit to whatever course of action the leadership chose to take in light of my sexual sin. I wouldn't have had any issue with disciplinary action or termination but it never came. It could be a point of debate for some, but the way the leadership handled things in my case is the way I hope they approach future cases that come to light the way mine did. I believe that the fact that I came forward of my own accord, seeking the administration's support, played a role in how they dealt with my situation. I know of other pastors who have opened up to their leadership about a porn problem, seeking help, and receiving support. Some organizations are offering to pay for counseling and other support services if their pastors demonstrate repentance and an authentic desire for recovery. I believe this is a healthy and restorative way to approach this issue as pastors who struggle come forward and confess problems with pornography.

I realize that not all revelations of sexual sin can be handled in that way. Obviously the viewing of child pornography or instances of child sexual abuse by pastors is criminal, as it is for anyone. Beyond the mandated reporting that any pastor, church, or school must do, this activity exceeds the scope of the church's power to determine what should or should not be done to the pastor.

This past season on the ski slopes I did something quite reckless. Feeling pretty comfortable on a new set of skis, I decided to hit the terrain park. That's where the snowboarders and extreme thrill seekers hang out, effortlessly gliding across beams, rails, and ramps. One beam seemed fairly tame, and I thought it wouldn't create too many problems for me. On my first attempt I managed to ski across it quite easily. It was enormously exhilarating too. So on another run, with my confidence running high, I tried to maneuver over the slick surface. This time things went terribly wrong. One ski drifted off, which left me balancing on the other ski all the way across the top of the beam, with my arms flailing wildly. When I came to the drop-off, my other ski slid out from under me. I crashed hard onto my side, planting my face in the snow.

My experience on the terrain park represents an attempt to venture outside of my comfort zone. I paid a price, but it was well worth it. Perhaps it's time to try something different in your ministry—something daring, even a bit dangerous. It may be that God wants you to go to a new city and plant a new church. Or it may be that you need to open up your life to a fellow colleague. No doubt you run the risk of looking foolish, but it might be the very thing that sets you free.

---

[1] Gary L. McIntosh and Samuel D. Rima, Sr., *The Dark Side of Leadership*, p. 22.

[2] *Ibid.*, pp. 22, 23.

[3] Mary Southerland, "For Women in Ministry: Opt for Peace," *Rick Warren's Ministry Toolbox*, Issue 247, Feb. 22, 2006. www.pastors.com.

Chapter 13

A Different Story

"Story is the language of the heart."—John Eldredge.

"Here I am! I stand at the door and knock. If anyone hears my voice and opens the door, I will come in and eat with him, and he with me."—Revelation 3:20.

When you strike up a conversation with those of us from the South, you often get more than what you bargained for. To interact with people from the South is to hear wonderful stories. If you ever stop and ask for directions in a southern town, you'll get not only directions but a local history lesson as well. There are no passing conversations. If you engage us, then you'll have to endure a more in-depth conversation. The same is true for church people. Just get a group of members around a dining table after a meal, and you'll hear some stories!

Those too busy to be bothered with stories miss an important point: life is as much about the journey as it is the destination. Your journey and my journey may be different, but the story is the same. We've lost our way, and we're trying to find our way home. Along the way we've encountered joys, setbacks, challenges, even loss. Yet we're still on the journey. Some time ago the thought occurred to me that any journey worth taking involves a climb. We can be encouraged because God is at His best when we face this life's climbs.

Lance Armstrong is arguably the greatest cyclist ever, having won seven straight Tour de France races and having overcome cancer. His story is an inspiring story of comeback. Lance often made his move to the front of the pack when he hit the mountain stages of the famous Tour de France. In other words, when the race became the most demanding, Lance made his move. I'm convinced that God makes His move when we face the mountains in this life. When life becomes the most demanding for us, that is when we can rely most heavily upon Him. That's why Scripture says that when we are weak, He is strong.

Another thing about Lance Armstrong that made the difference in winning and losing was the amazing team around him. While they haven't achieved the same celebrity status, his victorious ride into Paris' Champs-Élysées would have been impossible without them.

So it is with you and me. A solid team is essential if we're going to live a life that's pleasing to God. That team is made up of the saints mentioned in the Bible: God's people—the church. The word saint almost always occurs in the plural form. For every believer, these saints become a source of strength and encouragement to face any uphill climb that we may encounter.

John Eldredge in his book *Epic* takes a quote from G. K. Chesterton: "I had always felt life first as a story—and if there is a story, there is a storyteller." If indeed our lives are stories, and I believe they are, then it's important to consider who the storyteller is. Left to ourselves, the story is likely to take a tragic turn that doesn't end well. But if we hand over control of the story to our heavenly Father and allow Him to begin a new chapter for us, our story will likely take a turn for the good—and it most certainly ends well. God longs to be the author of a different story in each one of our lives— a story not of brokenness and failure but of recovery and new life.

I love to tell how Christina and I received a wonderful gift. A member of our church turned in a check for $1,000 as a gift to my wife and me. I was completely blown away and wondered if this was some sort of mistake. Eventually the member came to me and said that God told him to give us the gift. I wondered if God could tell Him that every month! Since my wife and I have a date night every week, I decided not to tell her about the gift just yet. I planned a special surprise dinner at an elegant Dallas restaurant. I knew exactly where I wanted to take her—a restaurant called The Mansion on Turtle Creek, a place where the rich and famous often hang out. At the time, it was the only five-star restaurant and hotel in Dallas. I let her know that we would be going out and that she should dress up because it was going to be special.

When the evening came, we headed toward the restaurant in a very upscale section of Dallas. As we pulled into the semicircle driveway of the restaurant, we noticed expensive luxury cars parked all around. We were a little embarrassed to arrive in our family vehicle, a Plymouth Grand Voyager minivan with a missing hubcap. But the valets hurried to open the doors for my wife and me, which was also a little embarrassing when dead french fries and chicken nuggets poured onto the driveway! We made our way into the restaurant and were seated at a quiet, intimate table with hardly anyone else around. I could tell that Christina was a little shocked that we would be in such an expensive restaurant, especially since she manages the checkbook. So I finally let her in on the surprise. I told her that we had received a gift of $1,000 and that she could order anything on the menu she wanted.

That was all she needed to hear. We ordered our food and enjoyed a great time of connecting and sharing together. It was a magnificent dinner, and the food was exquisite. Had my wife not been there, I would have been tempted to lick the plate! It was just that good.

You and I have been given an enormous gift by God. The gift of life includes not only eternal life but life *now*. Life isn't meant to go to waste. It isn't meant to be squandered with pornography or other sin. The gift of life is meant to be enjoyed to the full. Yet it's easy to get pulled away, leaving that which is so good behind and settling for what Edward T. Welch calls "a banquet in the grave." God's gift to us was expensive—it cost Him His only Son. That's why in Revelation 3:20 God says, "I stand at the door and knock. If anyone hears my voice and opens the door, I will come in and eat with him, and he with me." God calls us to fullness of life through intimacy and connection with Him. You don't want to leave one morsel on the plate!

Don't let pornography be the final chapter in your life. God is ready to turn things around and make you a champion defined by courage and endurance. It isn't God's plan that we remain stuck. Rather, He promises to raise us up to new heights. Like the psalmist says, "I waited patiently for the Lord; he turned to me and heard my cry. He lifted me out of the slimy pit, out of the mud and mire; he set my feet on a rock and gave me a firm place to stand. He put a new song in my mouth, a hymn of praise to our God. Many will see and fear and put their trust in the Lord" (Psalm 40:1–3).

This story ends the way yours will—with a restored walk and a testimony to share. God has already written the final chapter of our story so that we can live this life with great expectation and hope for the future. Our story ends at a party, where we're seated around a table at the marriage supper of the Lamb. Seated around that table will be many who limped through this life broken and tattered, but you won't be able to tell because we'll all be whole, complete, and new. We'll enjoy a magnificent time of intimacy with our Savior and Redeemer—"happily ever after." Journey over.

The end.

The beginning.

---

* John Eldredge, *Epic,* p. 5.

RESOURCES

The resources and advice listed here are to provide information for those seeking help. However, many of the resources (books, Web sites, workshops, speakers) do not reflect the doctrinal views of the Seventh-day Adventist Church. These Web sites are not intended in any way to be or to imply an endorsement on the part of Review and Herald Publishing, nor do we vouch for their content for the life of this book.

Web sites
- www.pureintegrity.org
- www.newlife.com
- www.pureintimacy.org
- www.xxxchurch.com
- www.pureonline.com
- www.protectkids.com
- www.purelifeministries.org
- www.settingcaptivesfree.com
- www.puredesire.org
- www.sexualrecovery.com
- www.contentwatch.com
- www.toptenreviews.com

- www.sexhelp.com
- www.porn-free.org
- www.sexaa.org
- www.sa.org
- www.cp80.org

Books

•*An Affair of the Mind*, by Laurie Hall

•*Every Man's Battle: Winning the War on Sexual Temptation One Victory at a Time*, by Stephen Arterburn and Fred Stoeker; editor Mike Yorkey

•*Every Woman's Battle: Discovering God's Plan for Sexual and Emotional Fulfillment*, by Shannon Ethridge

•*False Intimacy: Understanding the Struggle of Sexual Addiction*, by Harry W. Schaumburg

•*Father and Son*, by Gordon Dalbey

•*Healing the Wounds of Sexual Addiction*, by Mark R. Laaser

•*In the Shadows of the Net: Breaking Free of Compulsive Online Sexual Behavior*, by Patrick Carnes, David L. Delmonico, et al.

•*Pure Desire*, by Ted Roberts

•*Sex Is Not the Problem (Lust Is)*, by Joshua Harris

•*The Pornography Trap*, by Ralph H. Earle, Jr., and Mark R. Laaser

•*The Sexual Man*, by Archibald D. Hart

•*The Game Plan*, by Joe Dallas

•*Think Before You Look*, by Daniel Henderson

•*Untangling the Web: Sex, Porn, and Fantasy Obsession in the Internet Age*, by Robert Weiss and Jennifer Schneider

•*Wild at Heart*, by John Eldredge

Workshops

- Every Man's Battle. For more information: